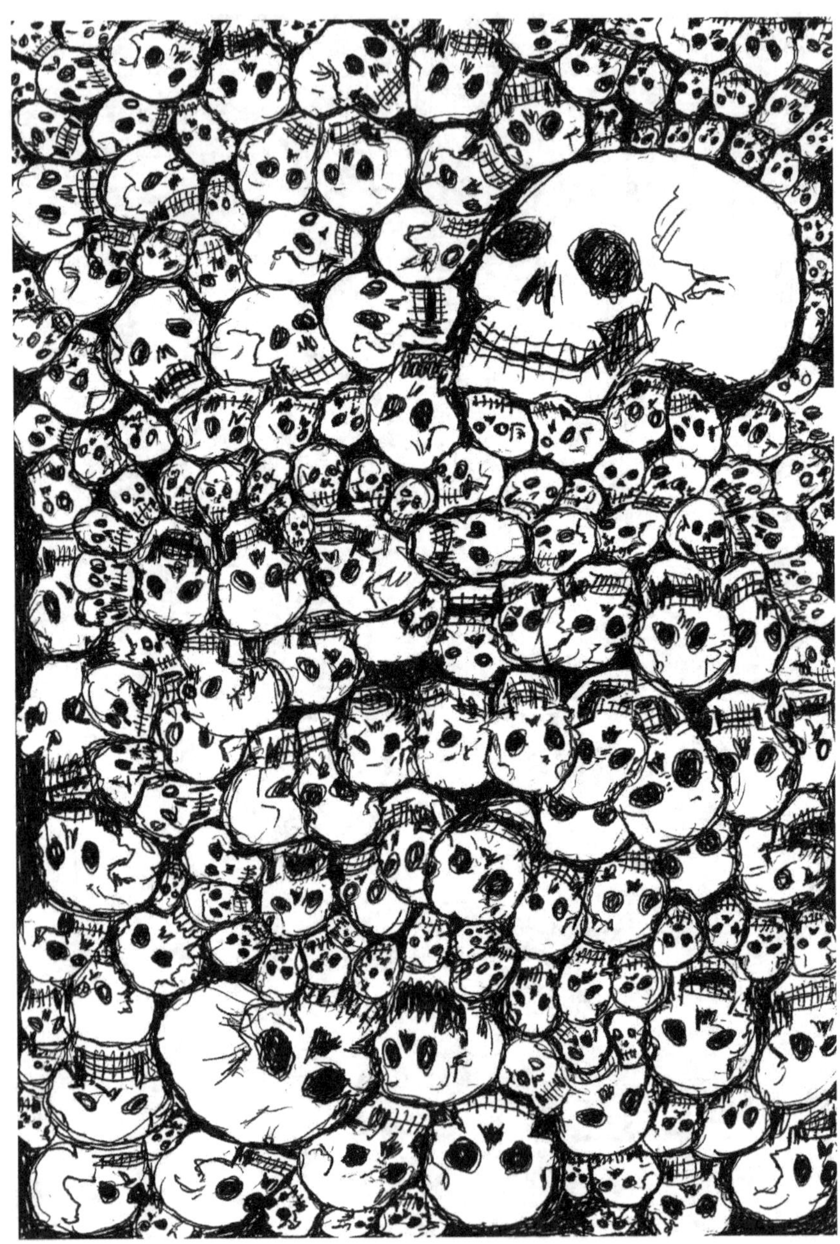

$&%#!!!

Art Collection # 3

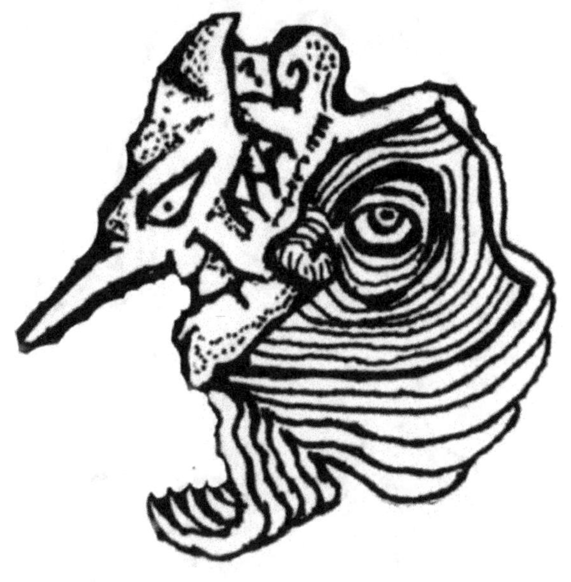

80 Small black & white drawings, scribbles & doodles

by

Eric C. Harrison

Circa 1987-2012

Marsh-Paw Press

2013

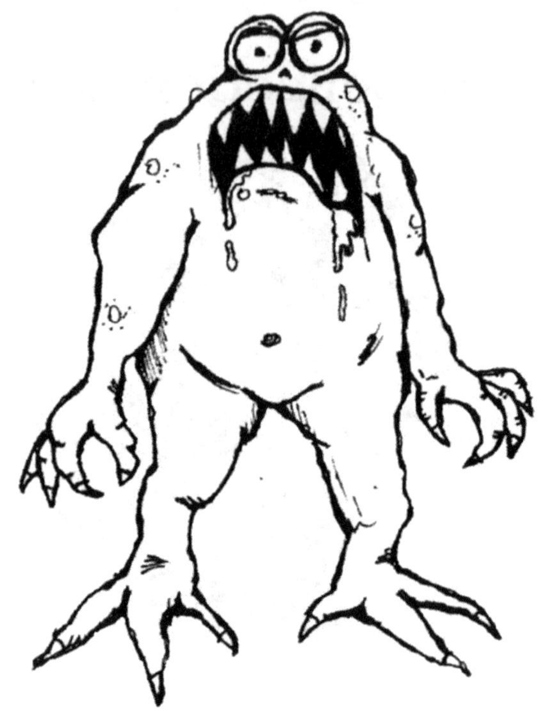

$&%#!!!

Art Collection # 3

80 Small black & white drawings, scribbles & doodles

ISBN 978-0-9888040-2-9

Published by Marsh Paw Press - January, 2013

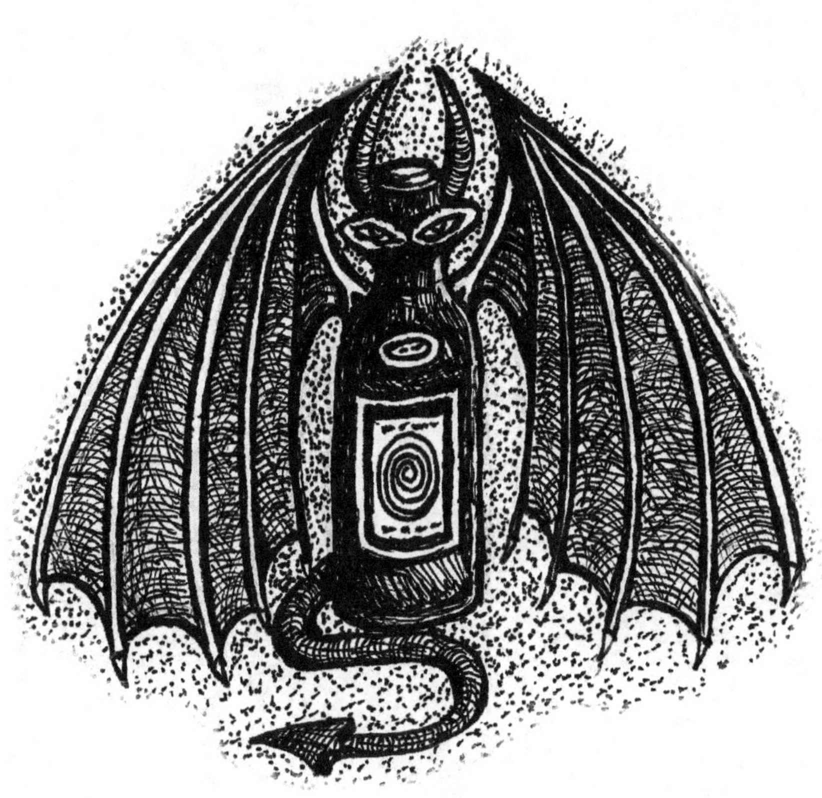

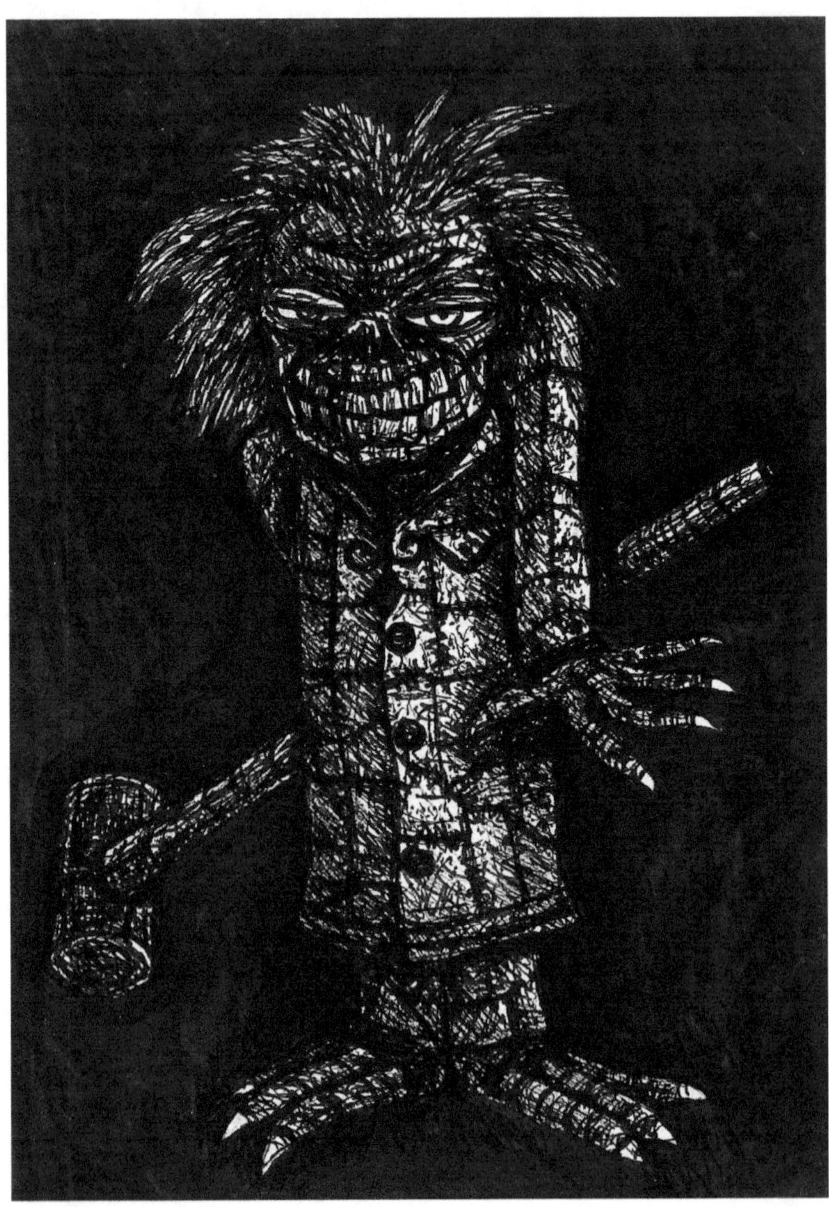

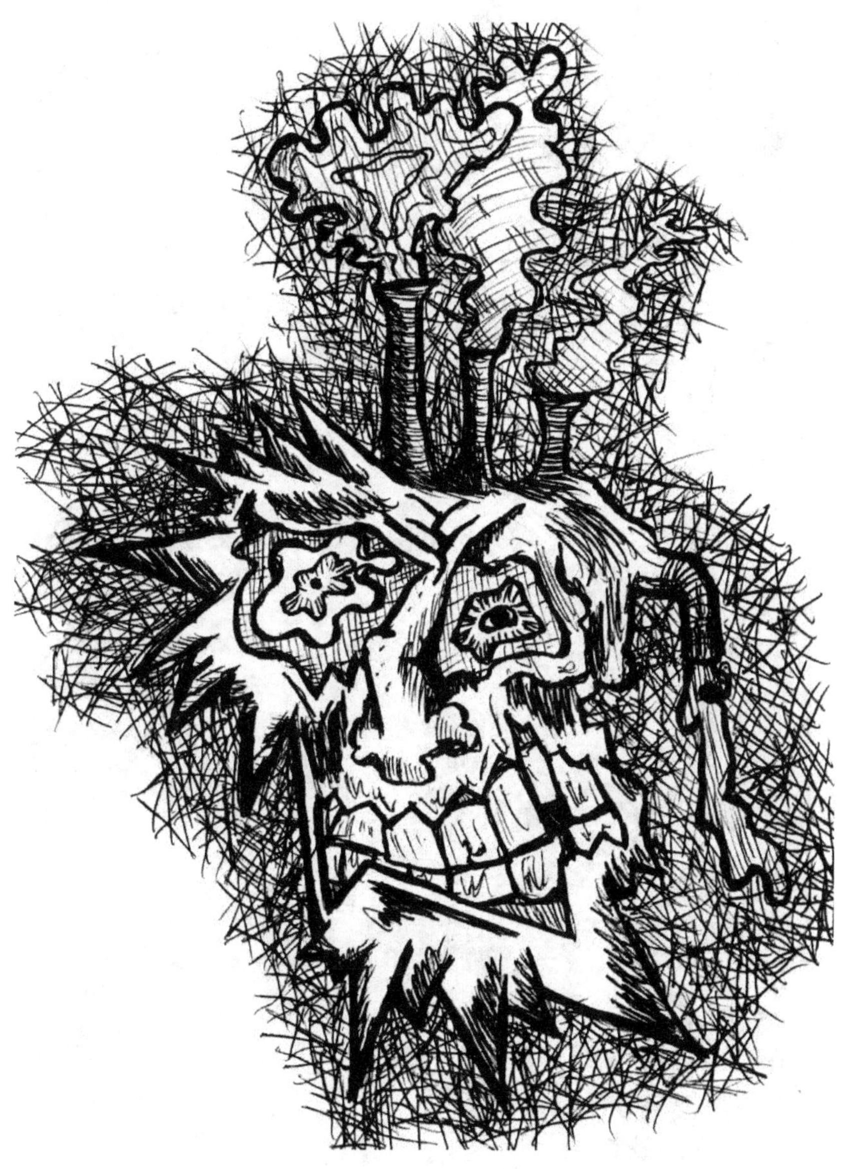

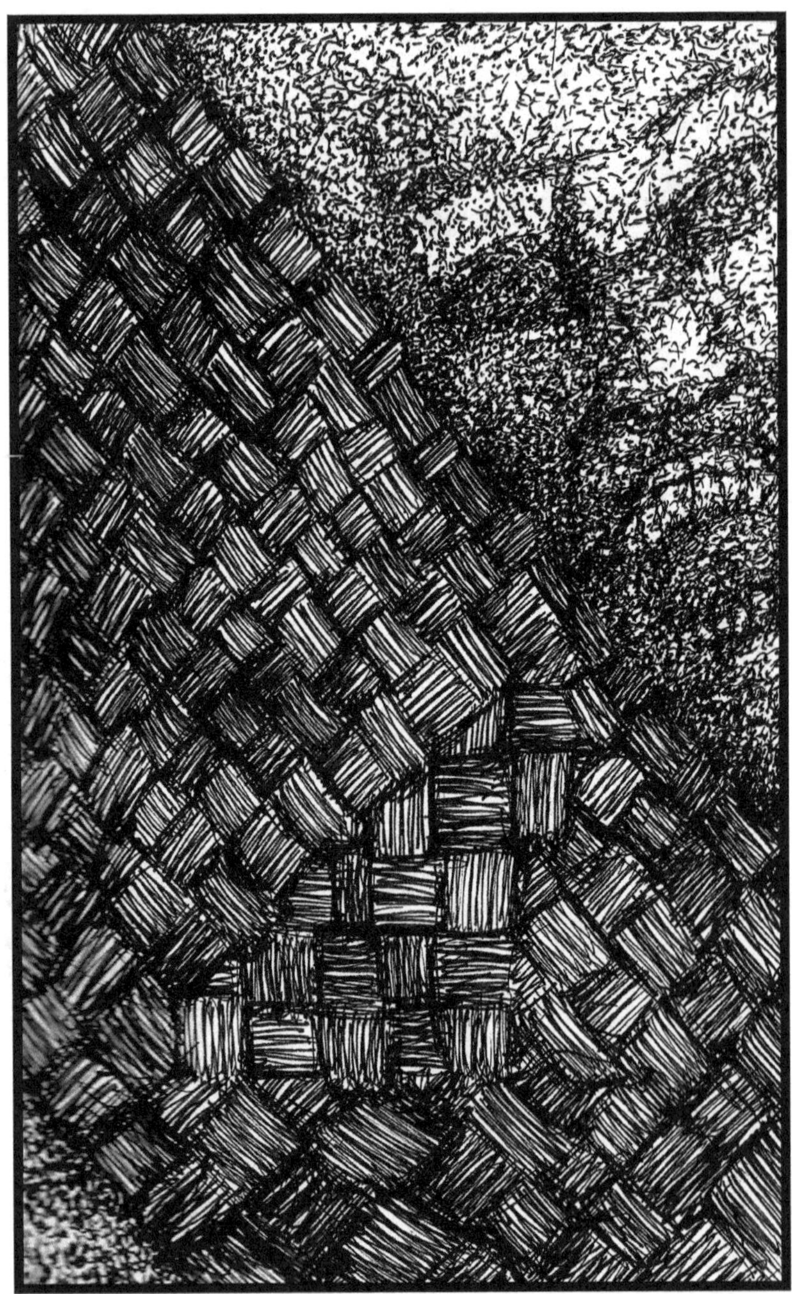

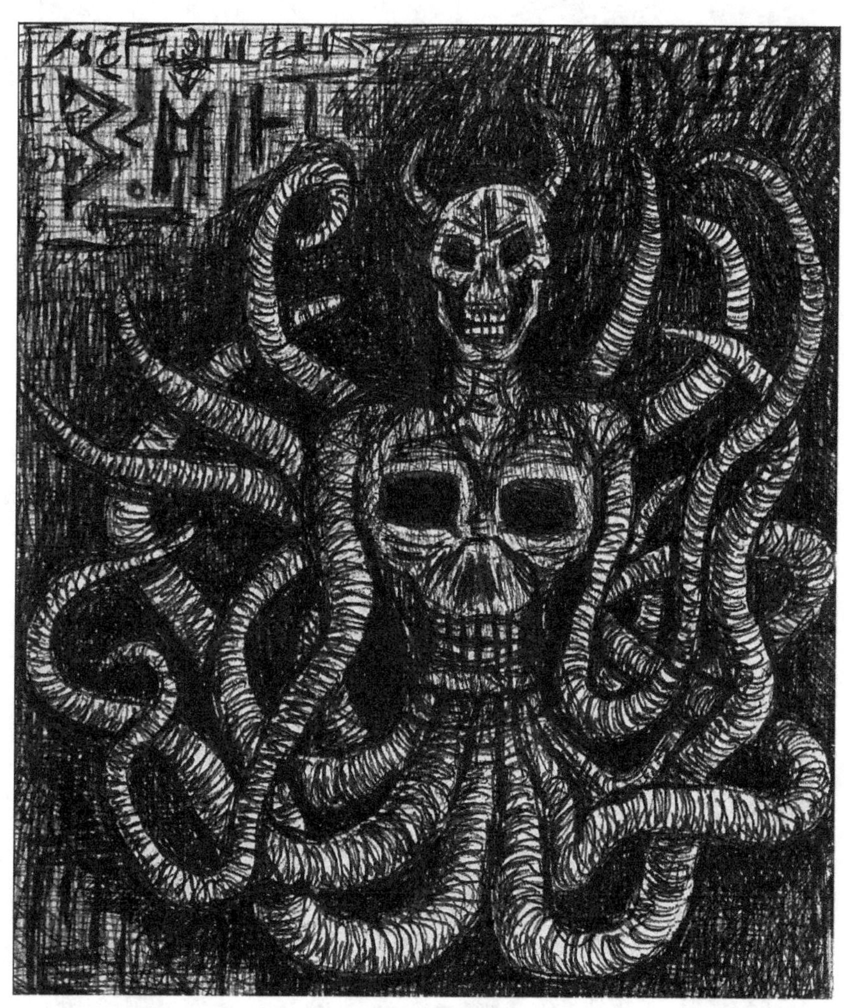

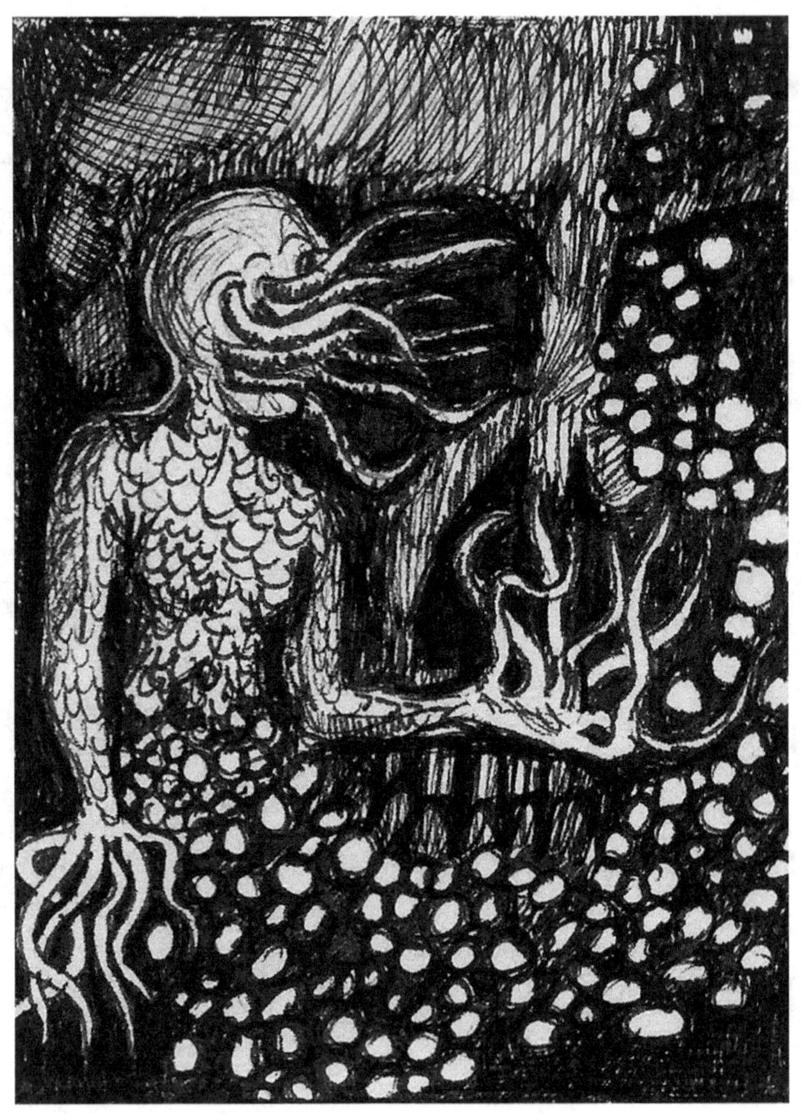

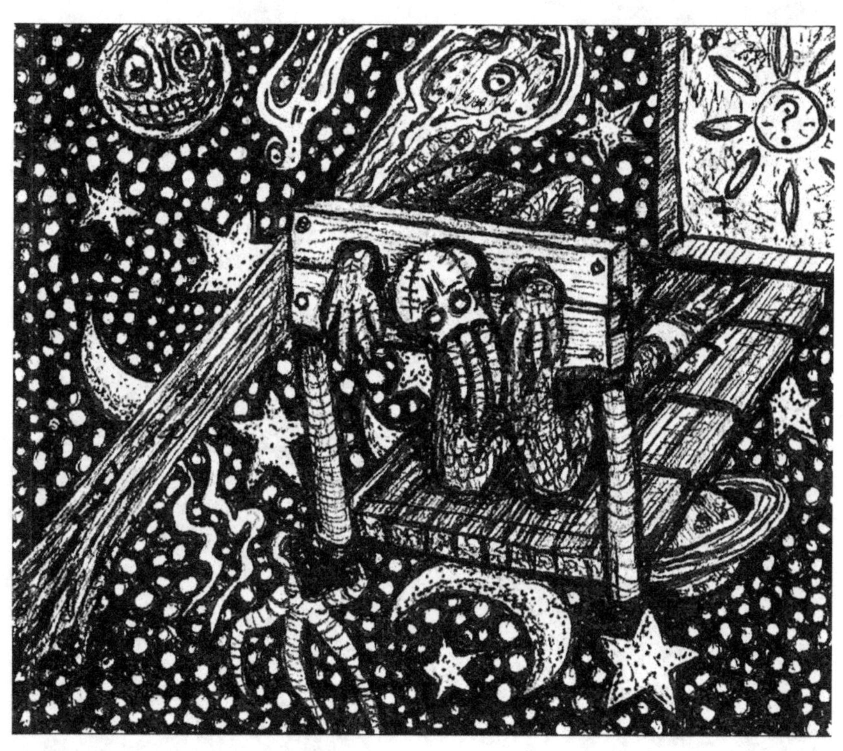

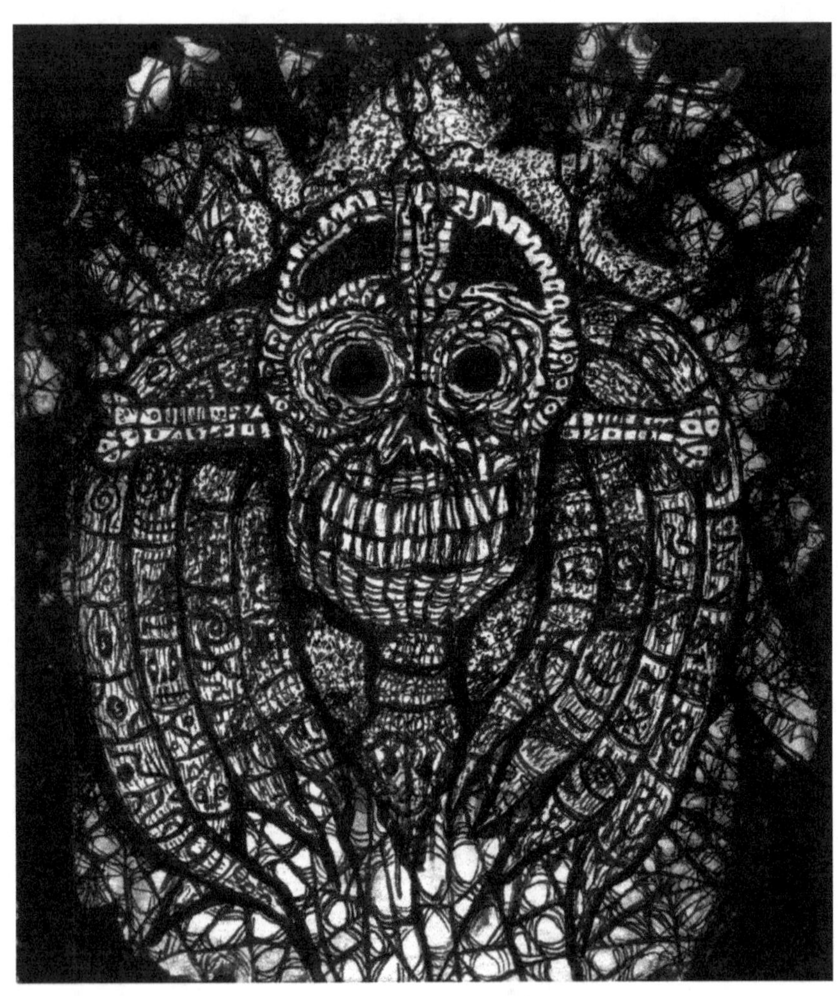

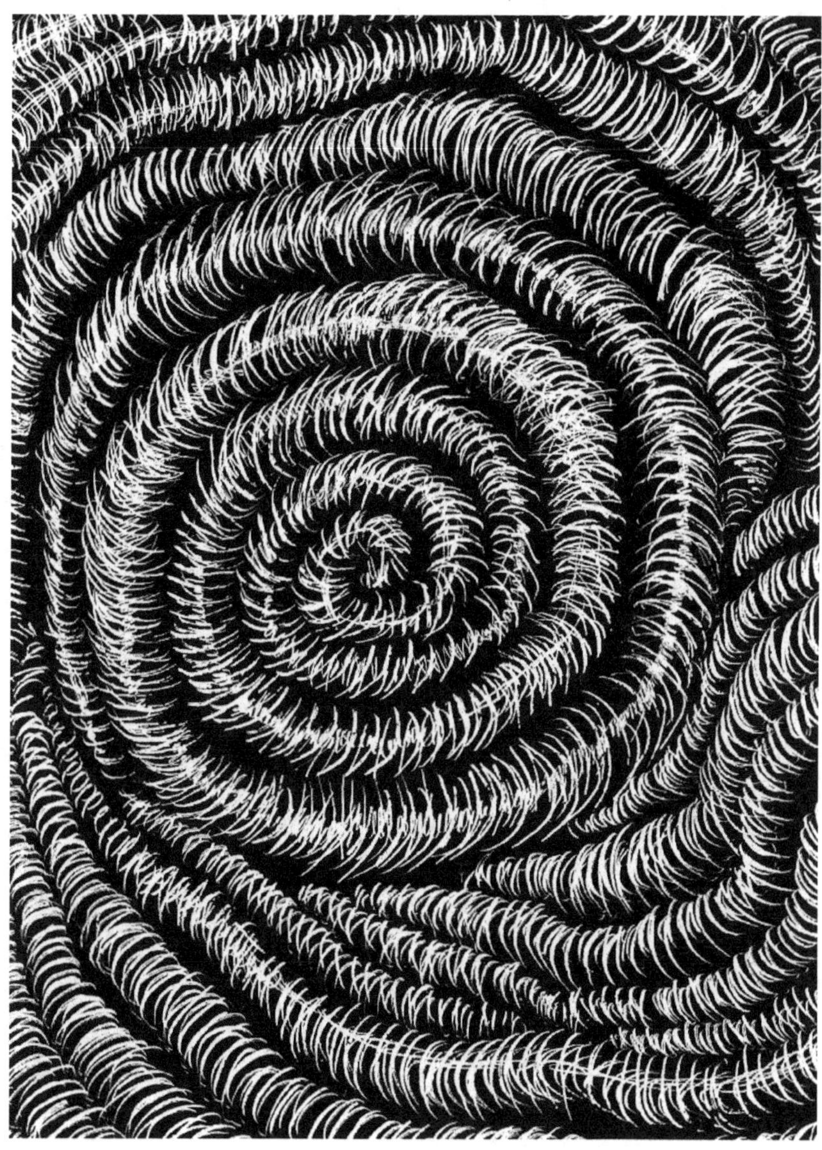

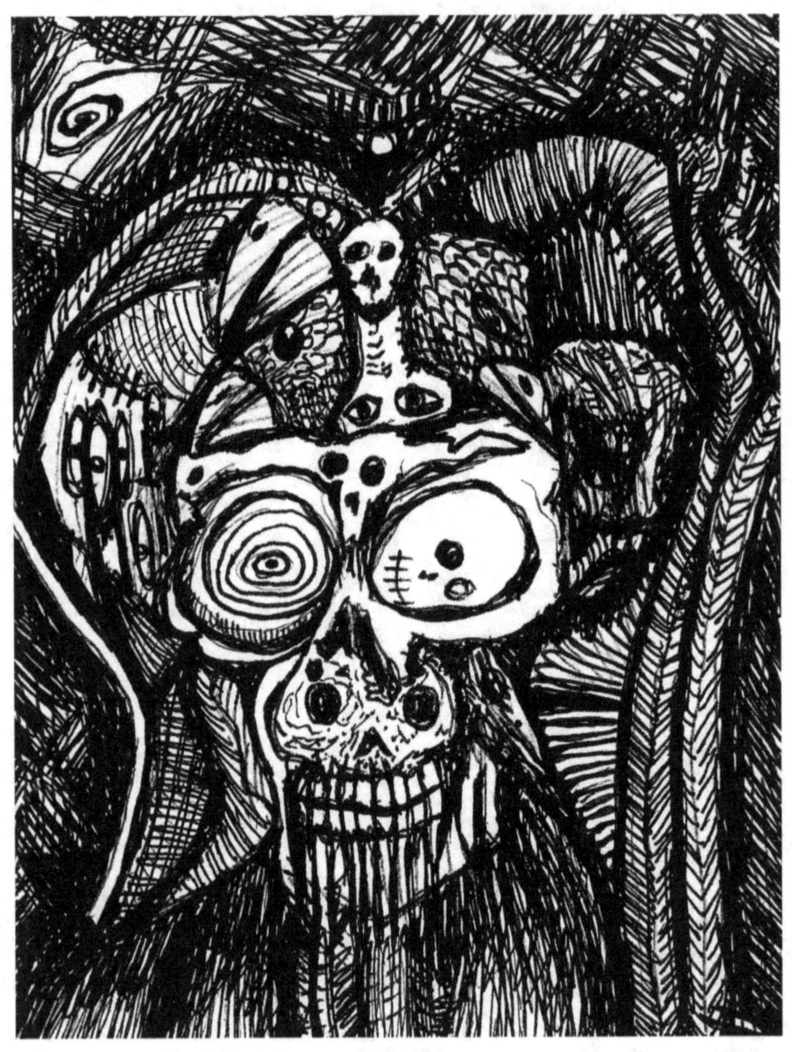

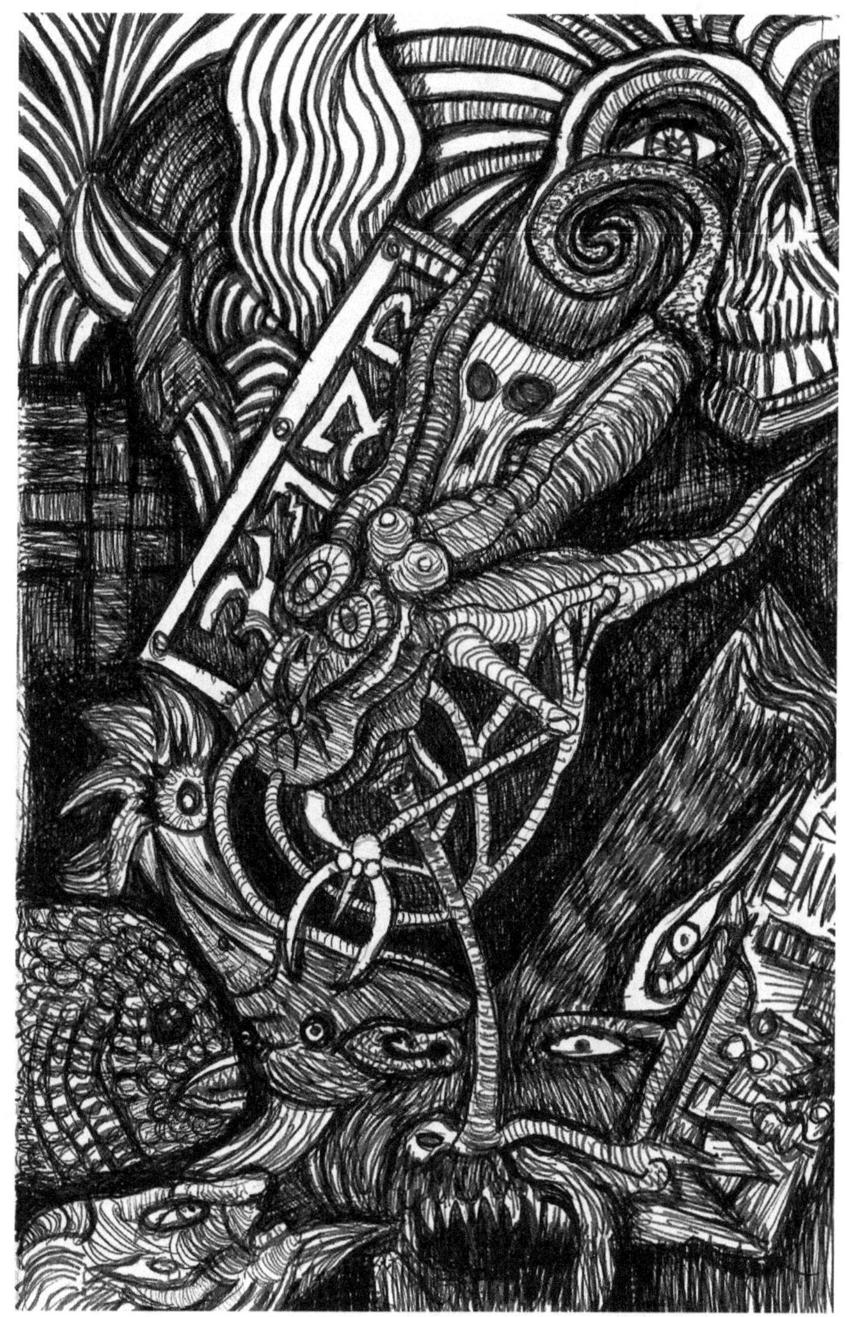

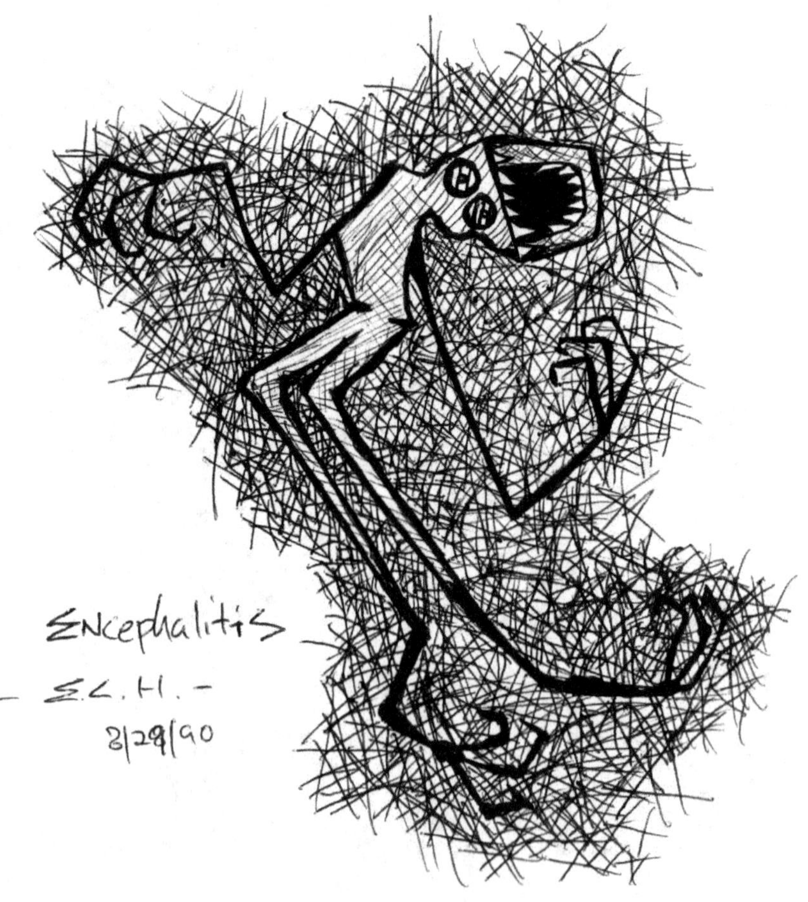
Encephalitis
- E.L.H. -
8/29/90

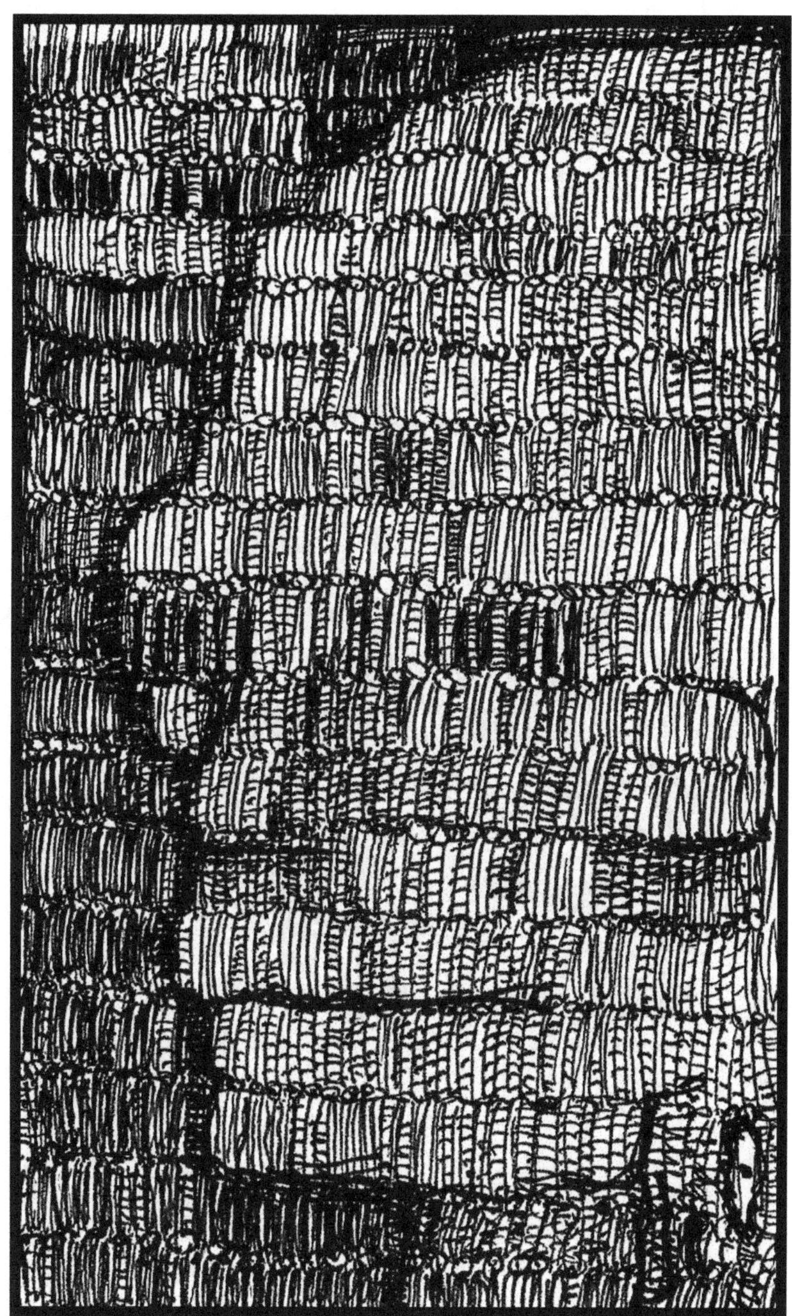

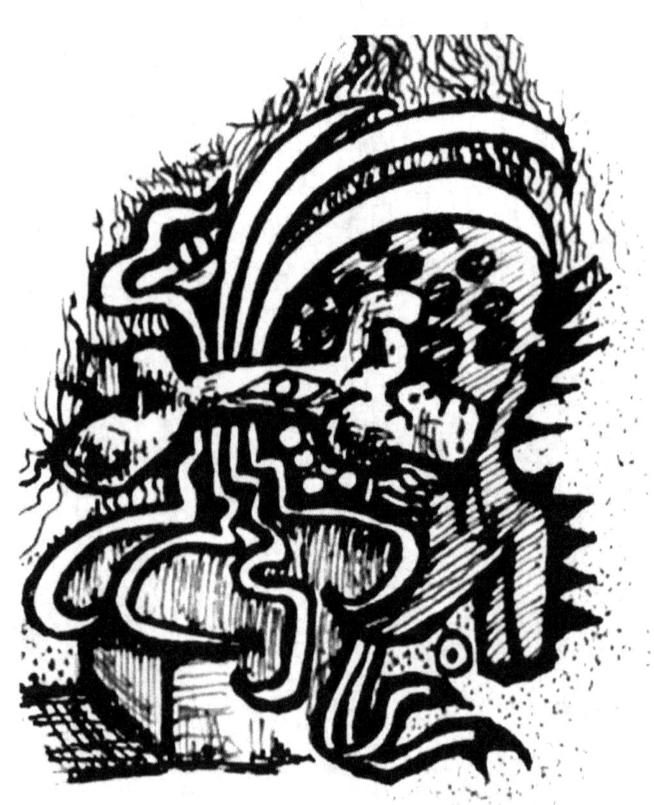

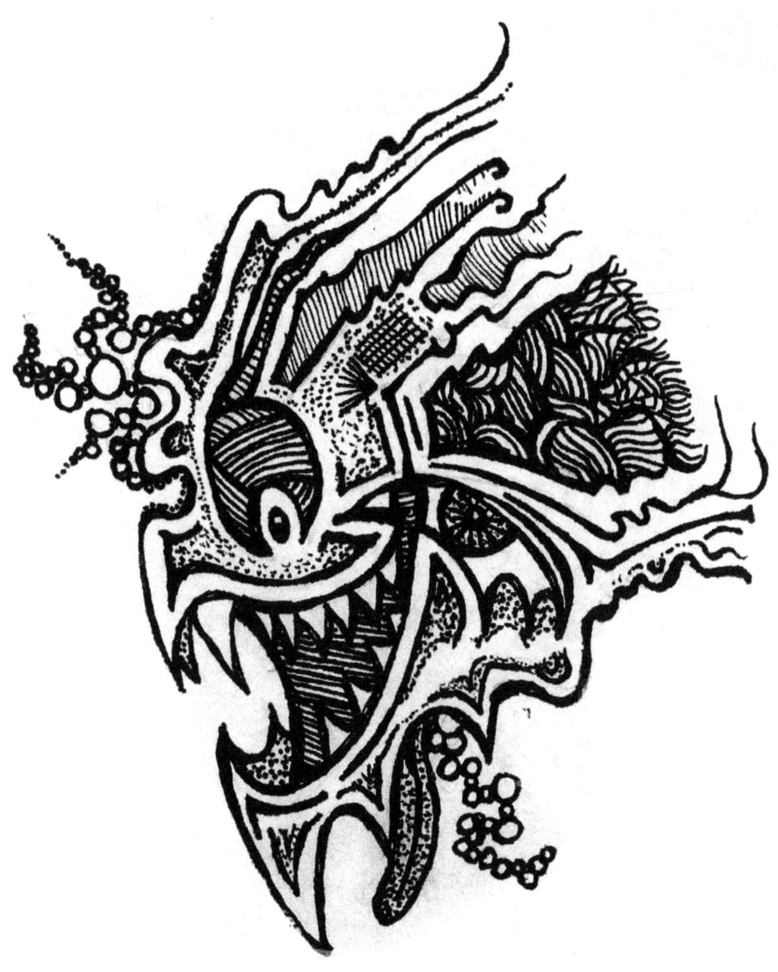

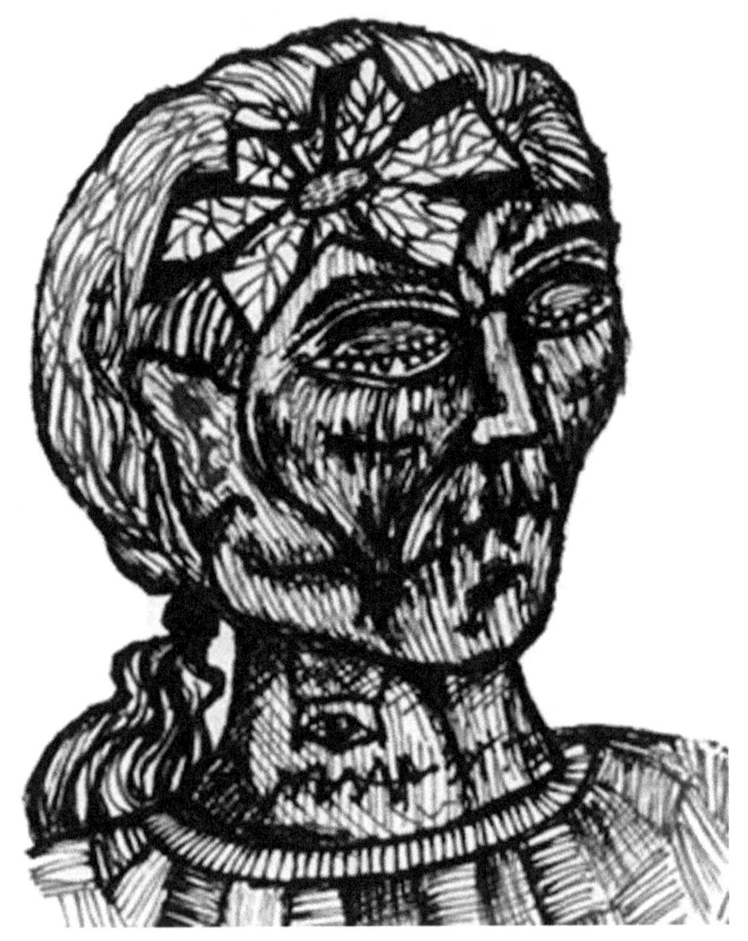

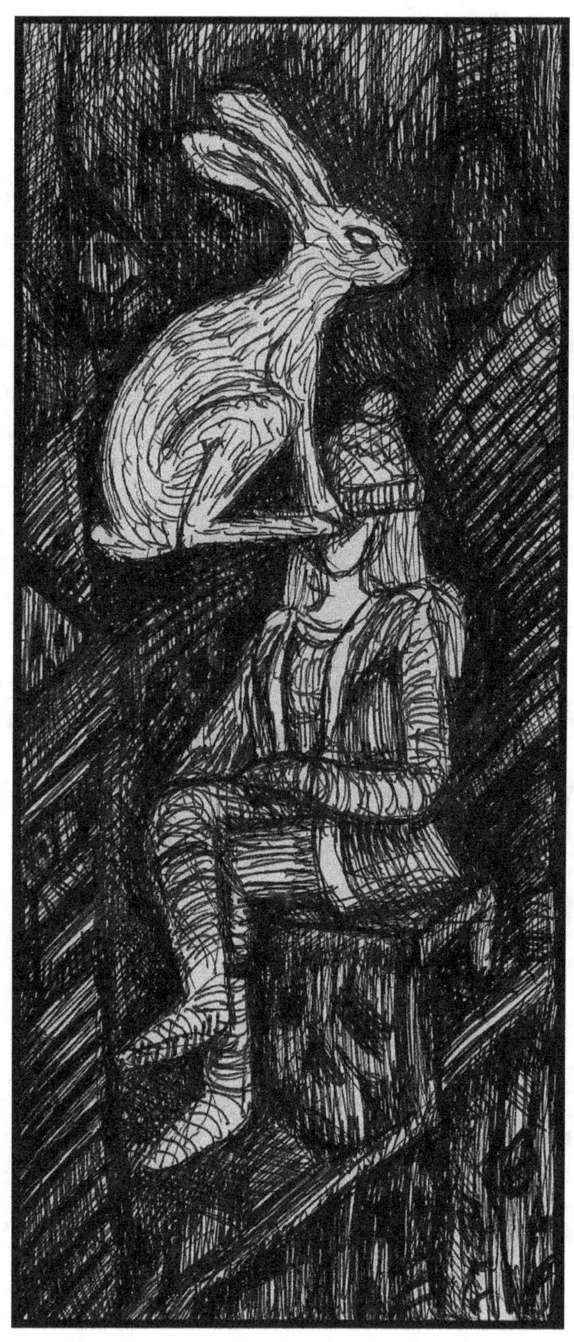

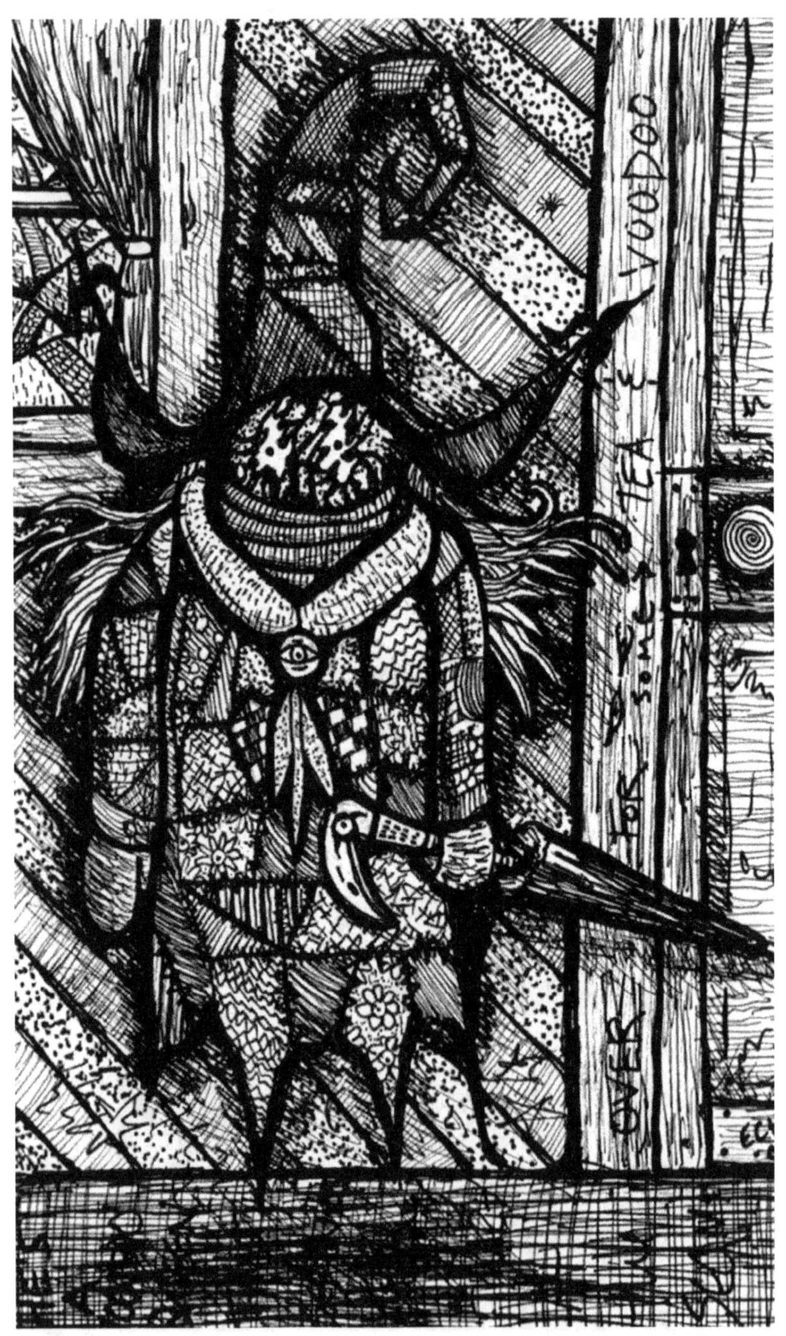
VOODOO
TEA
OVER

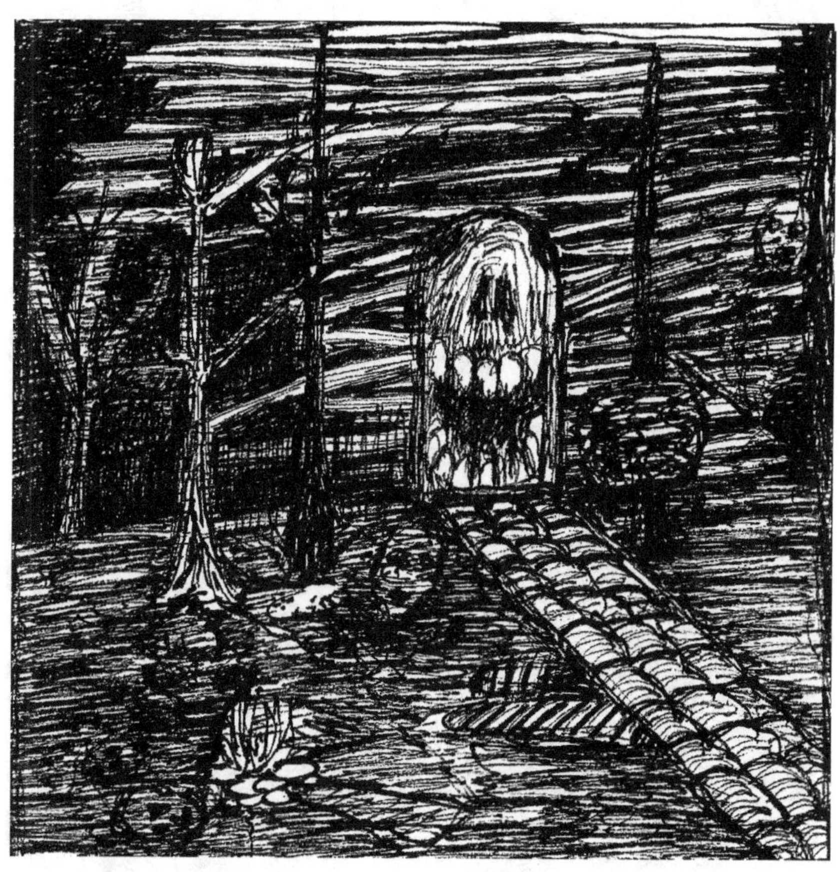

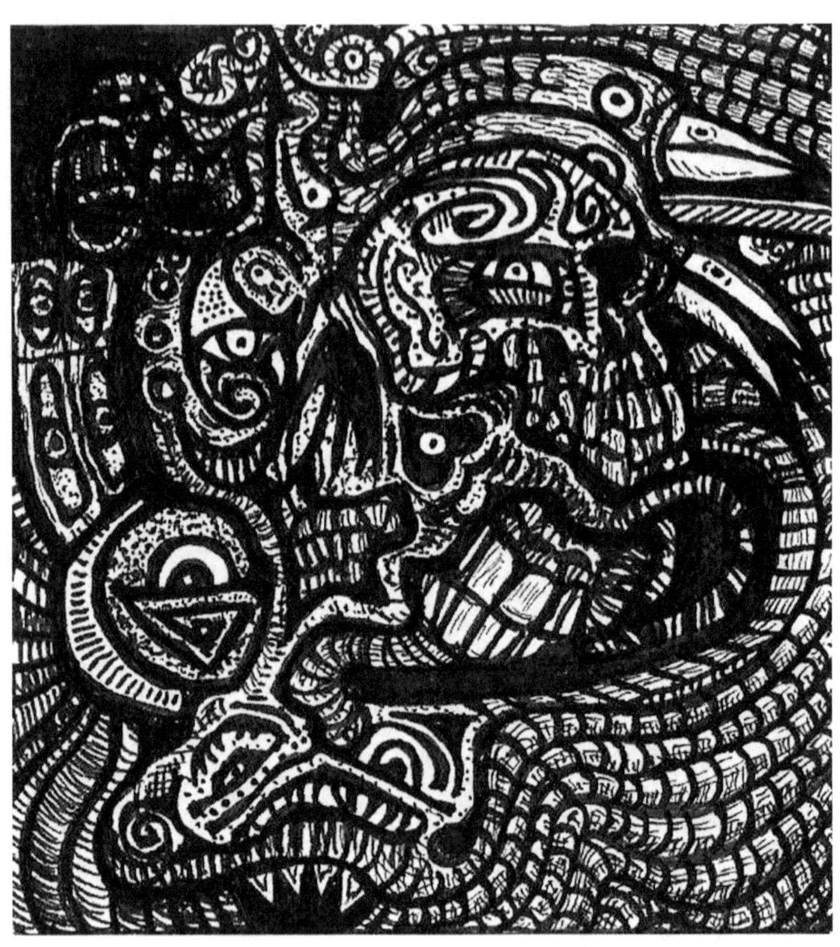

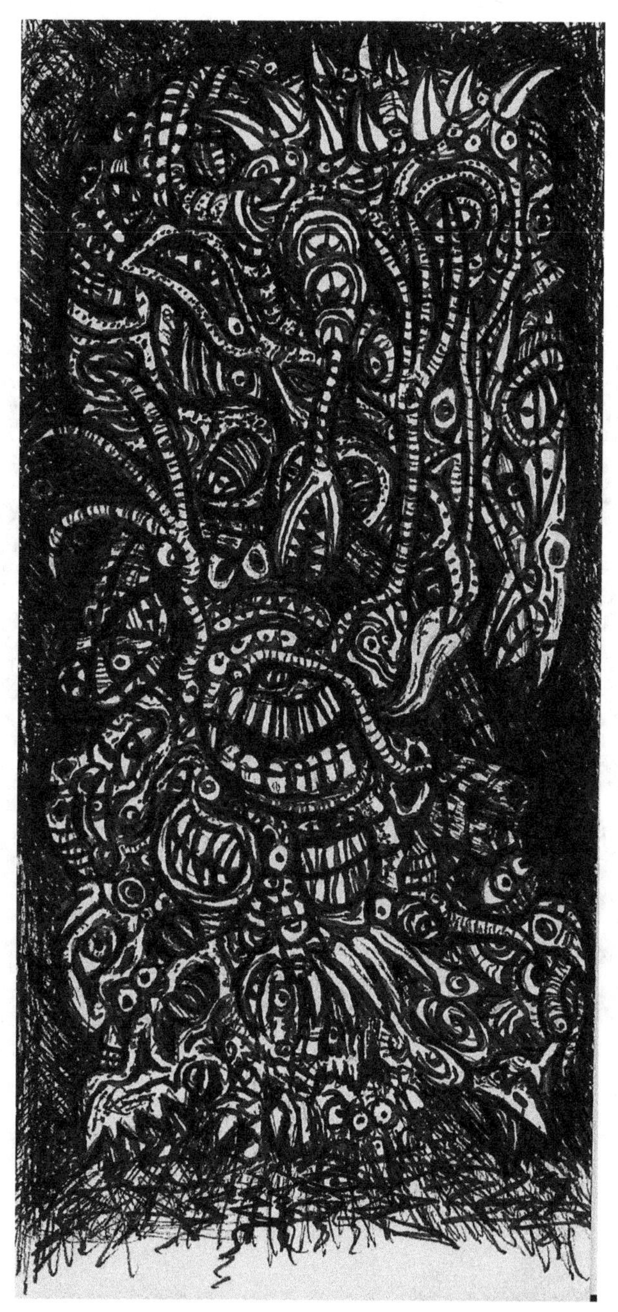

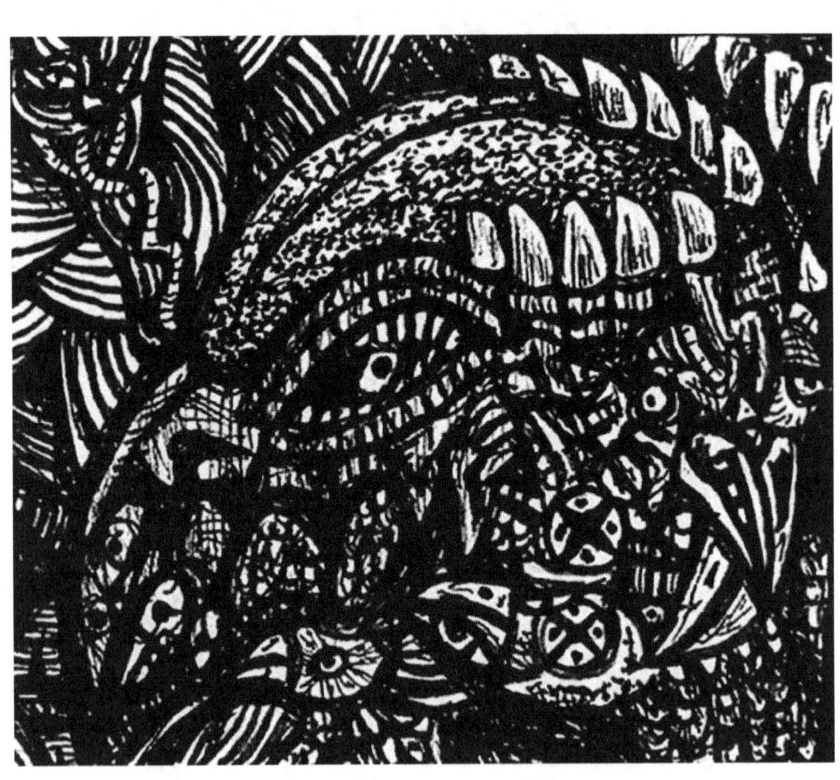

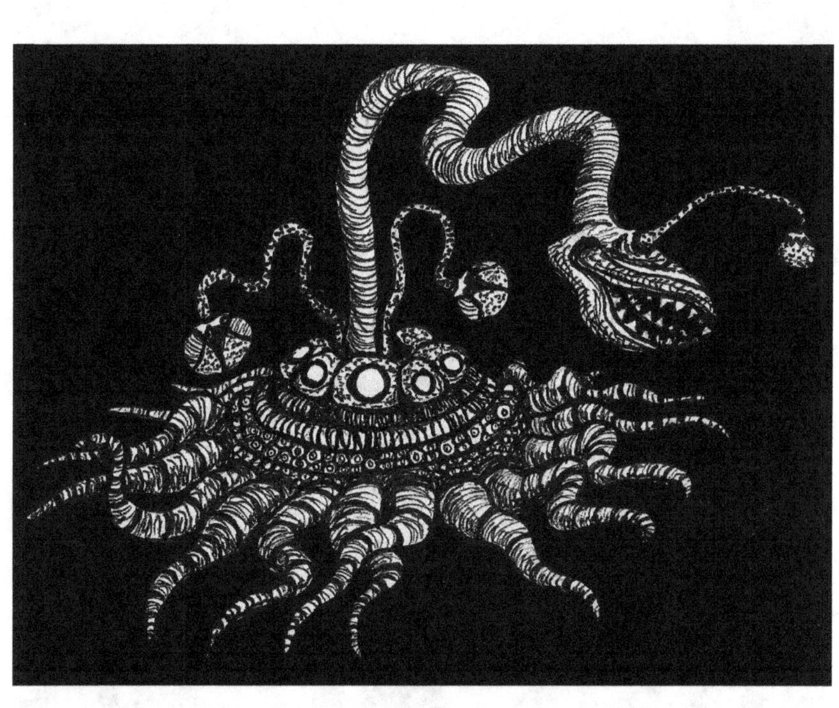

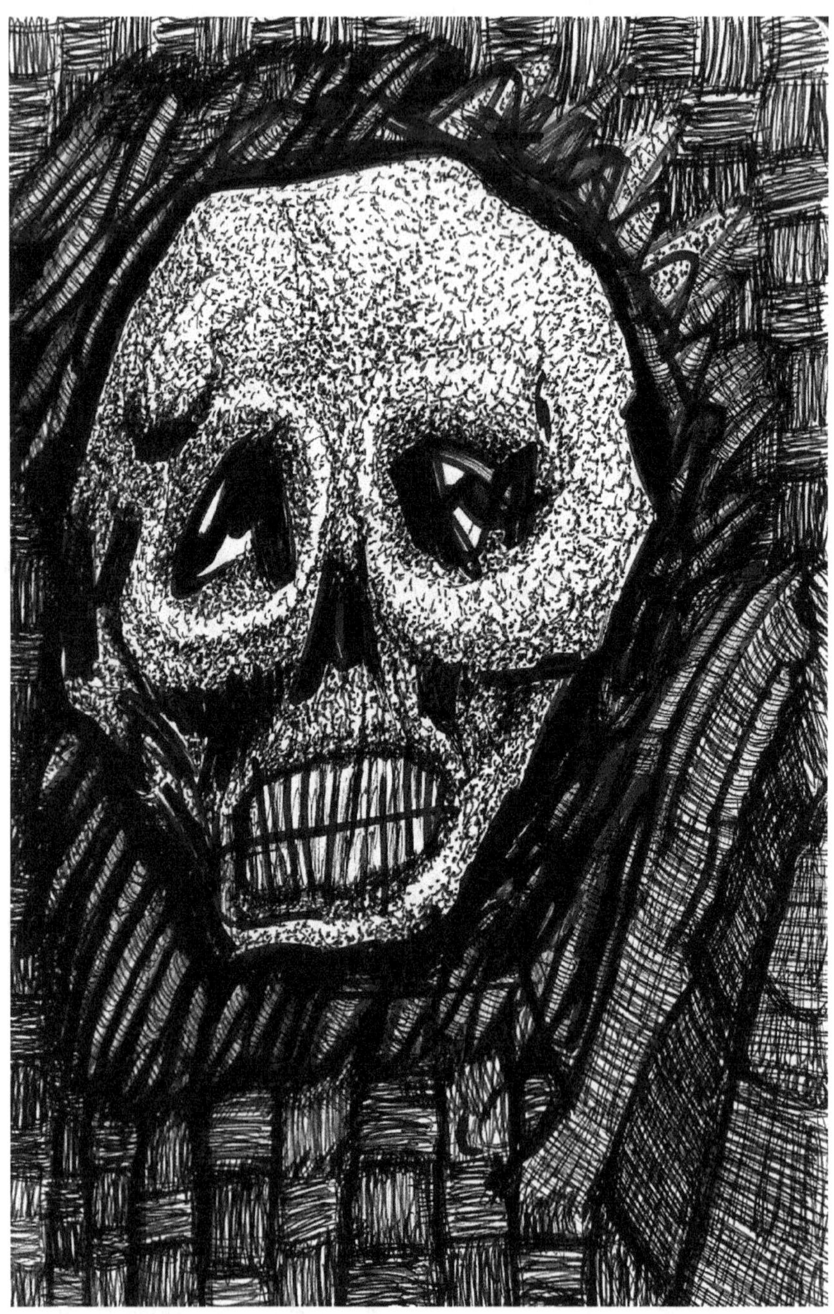

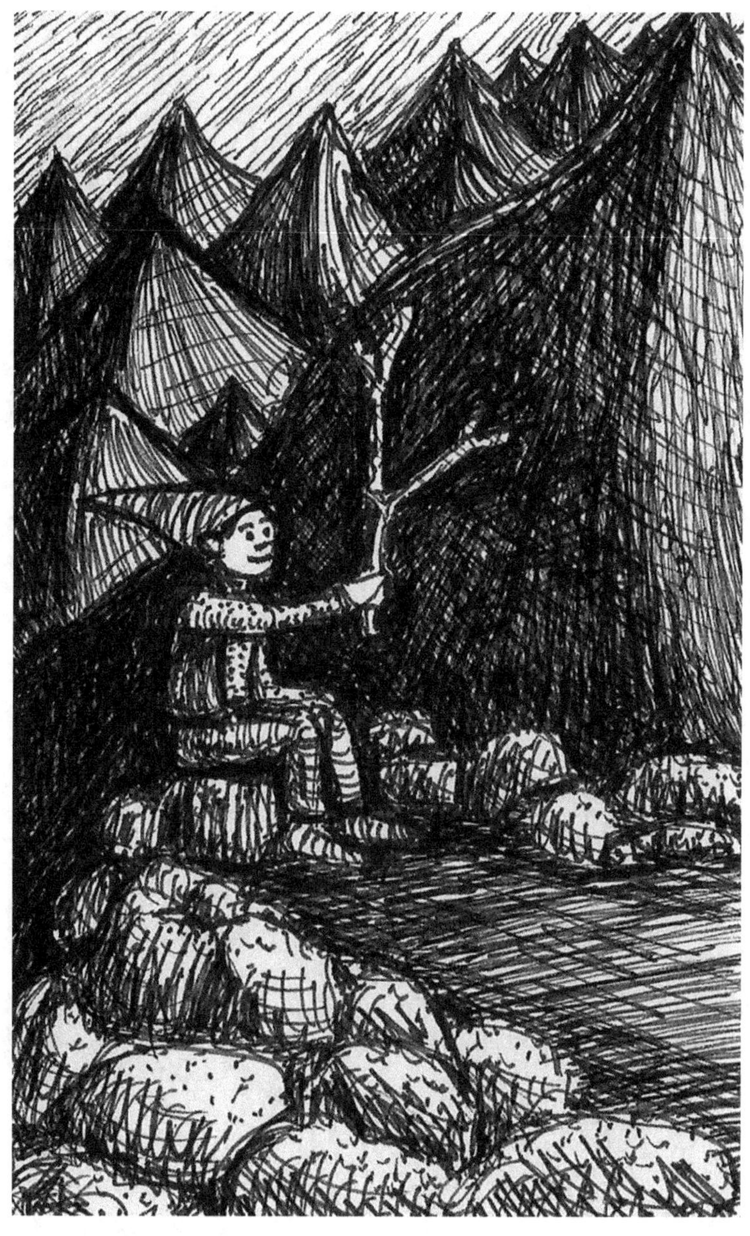

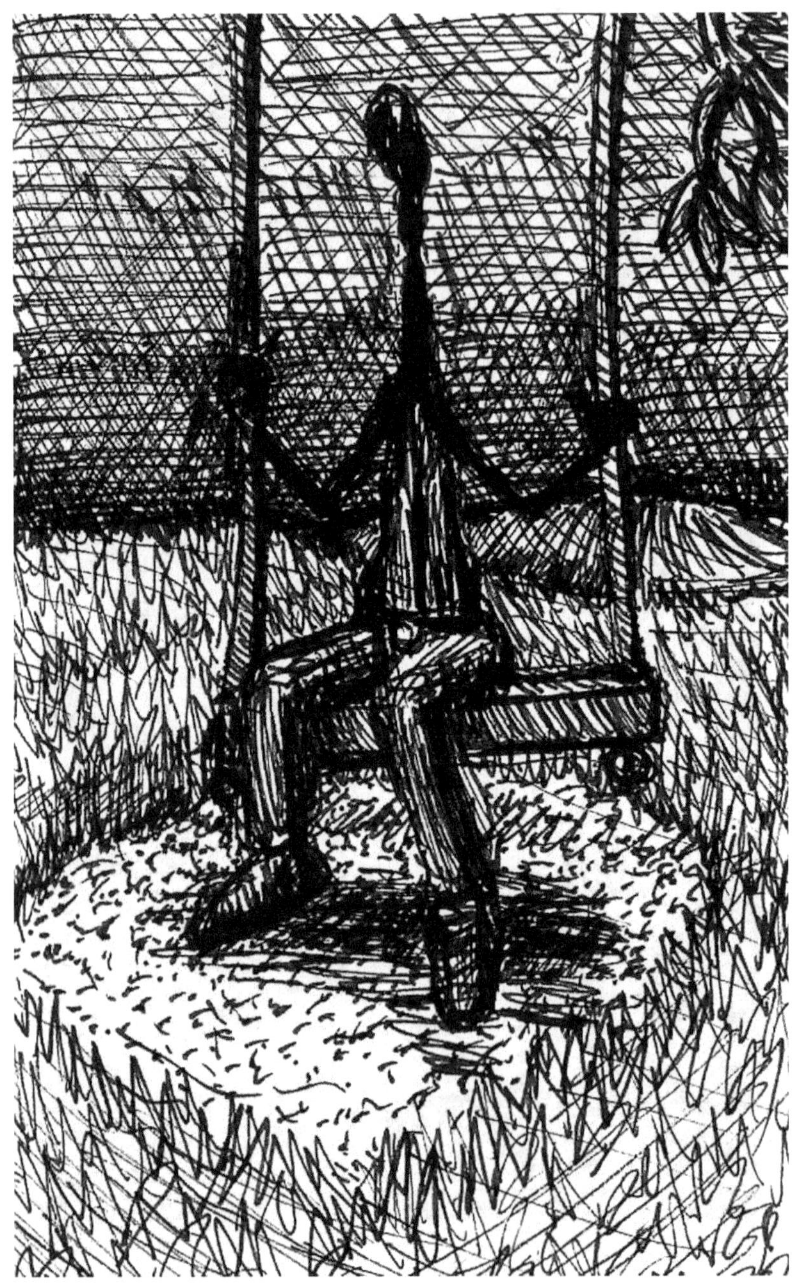

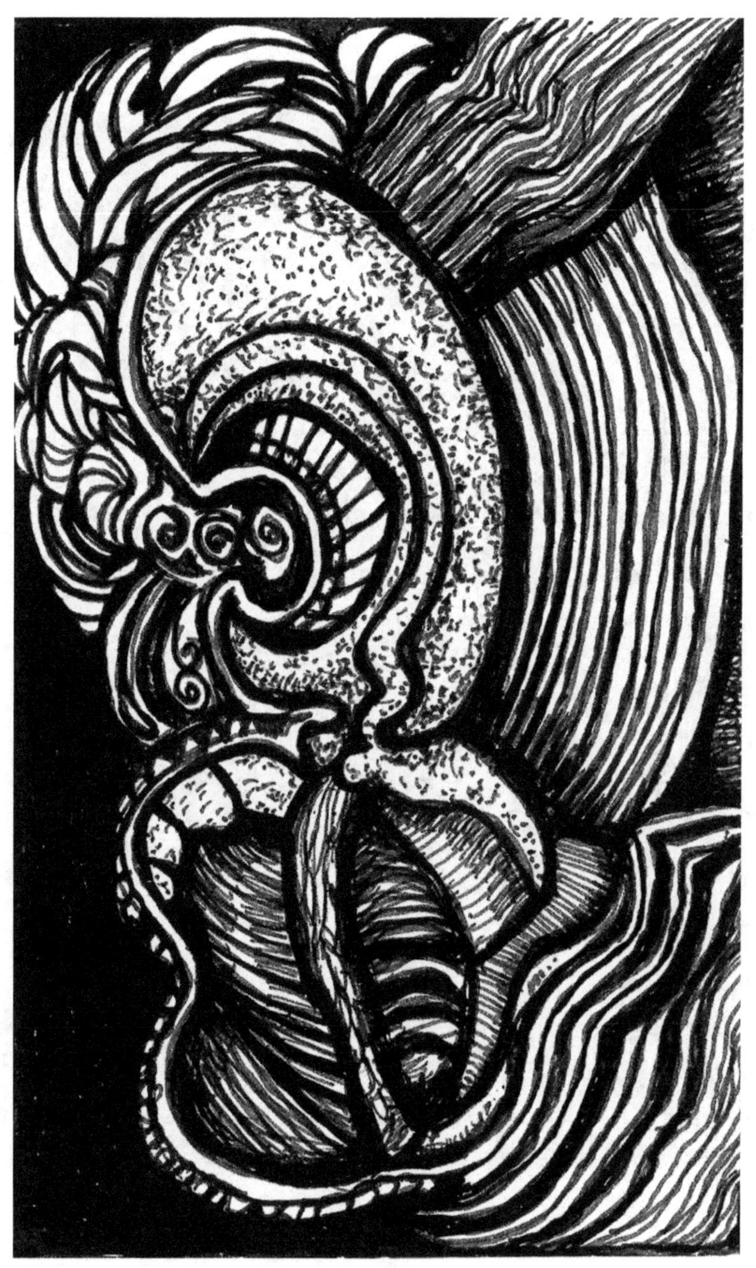

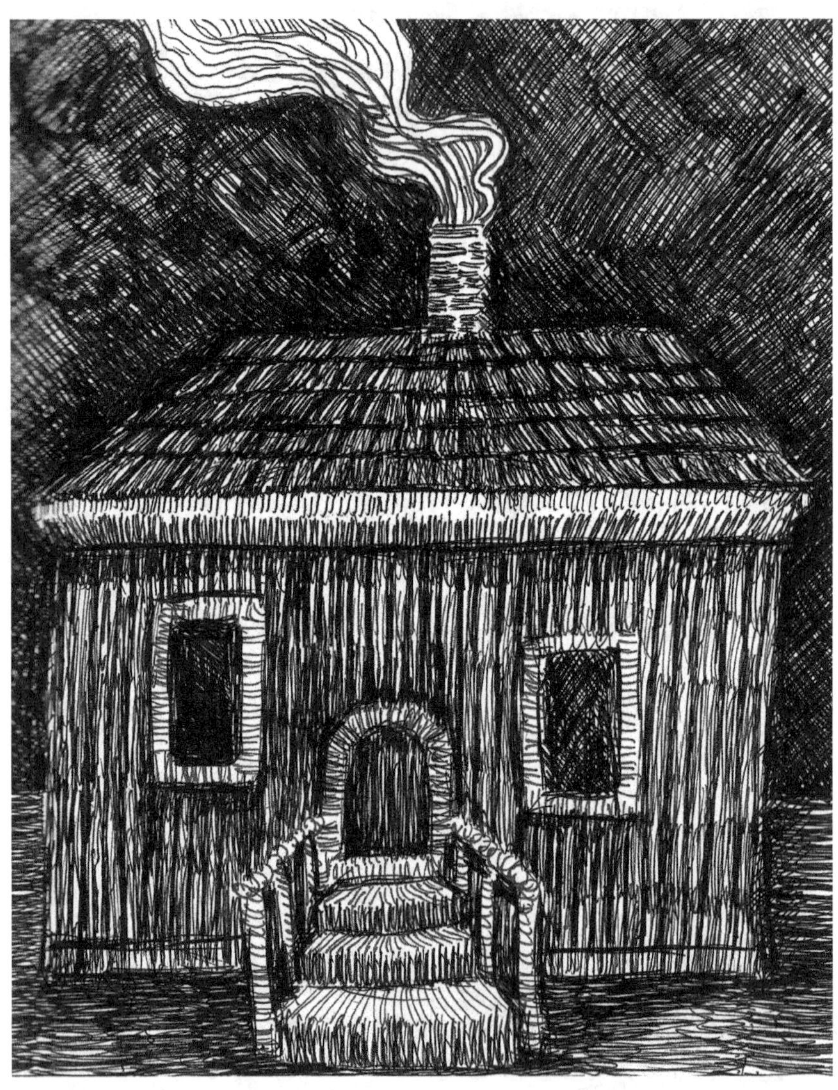

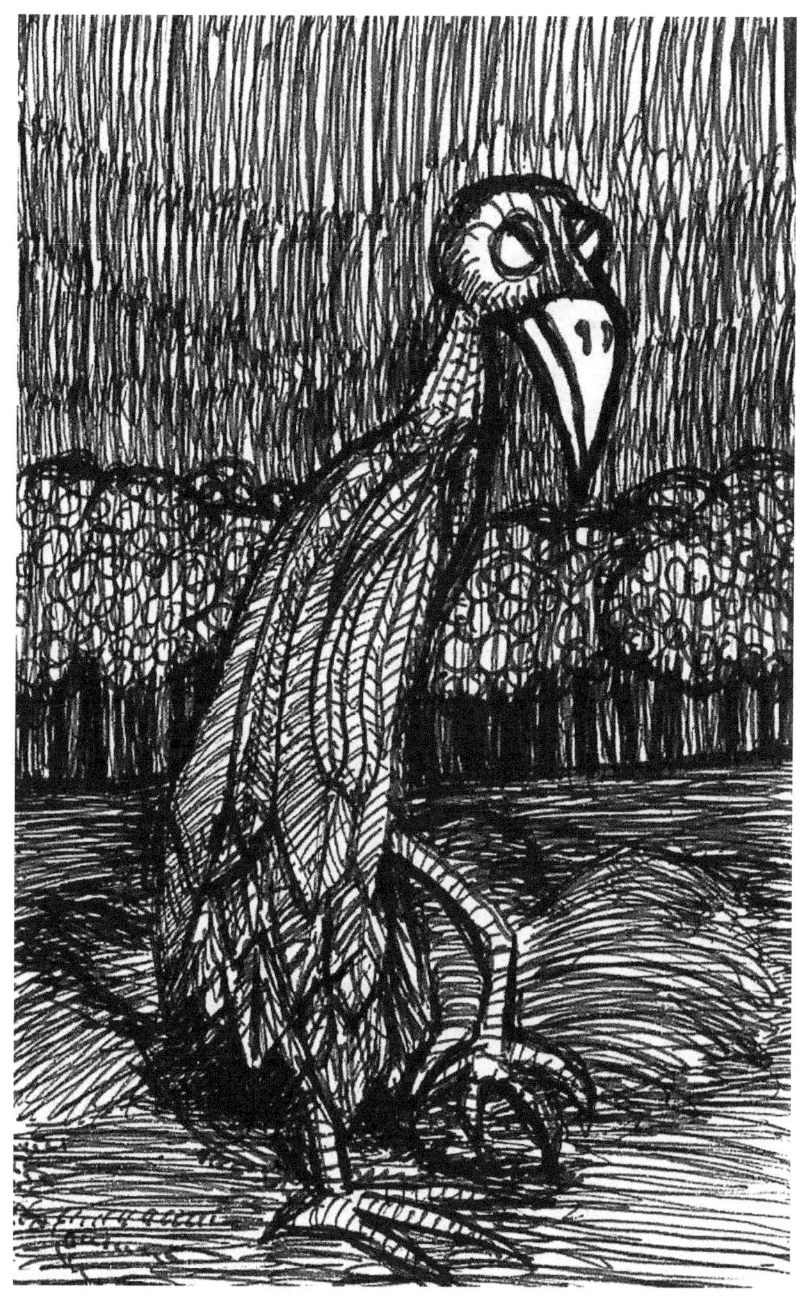

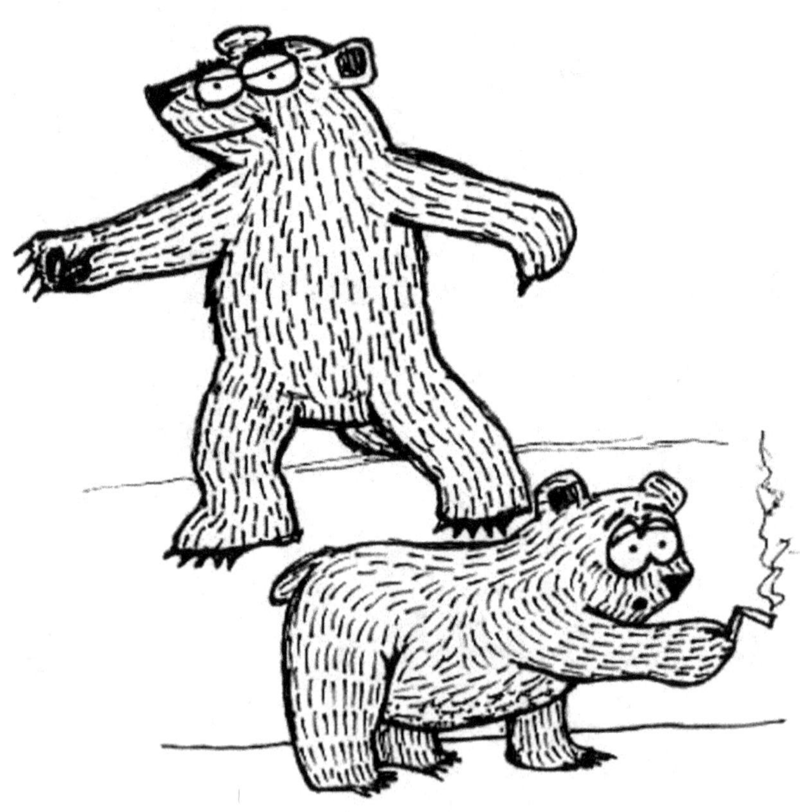

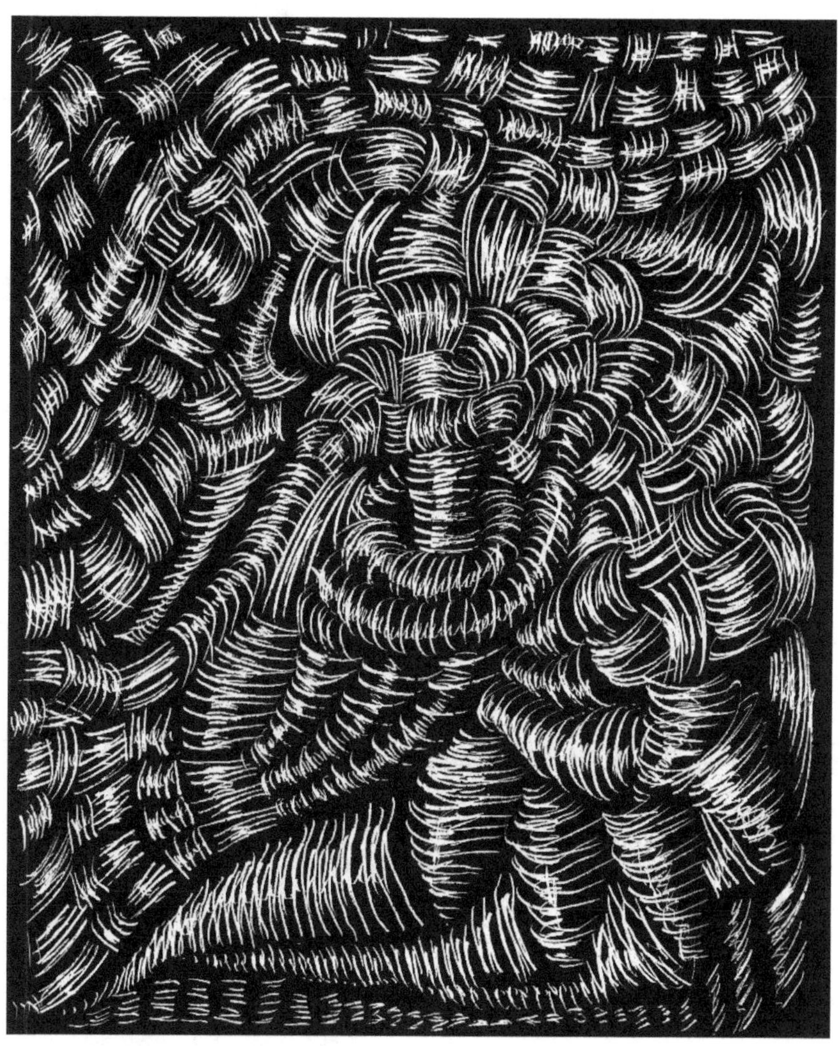

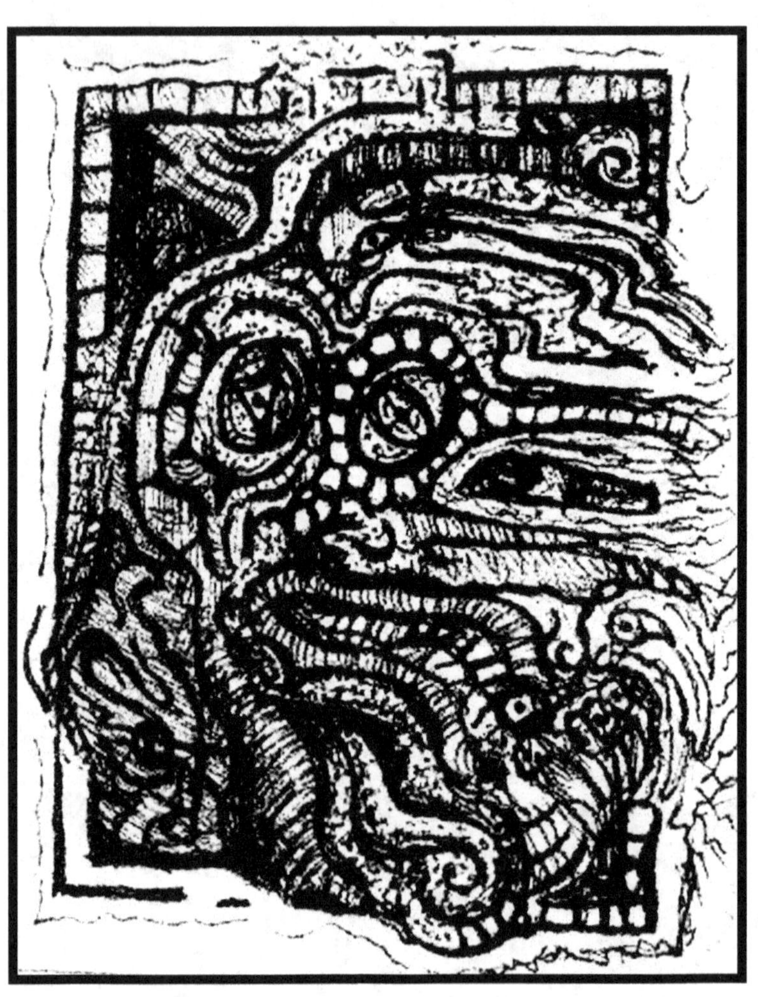

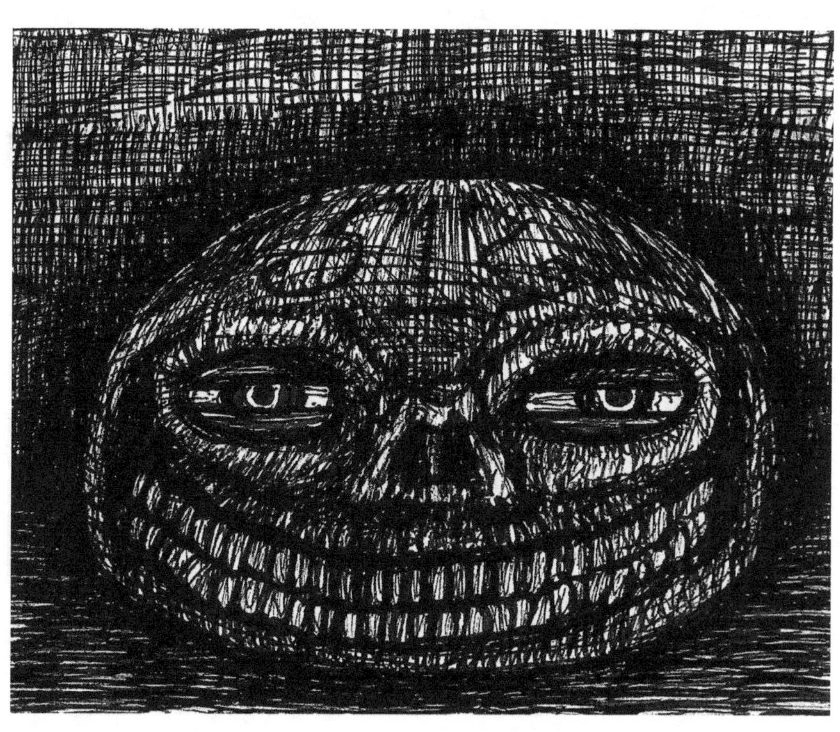

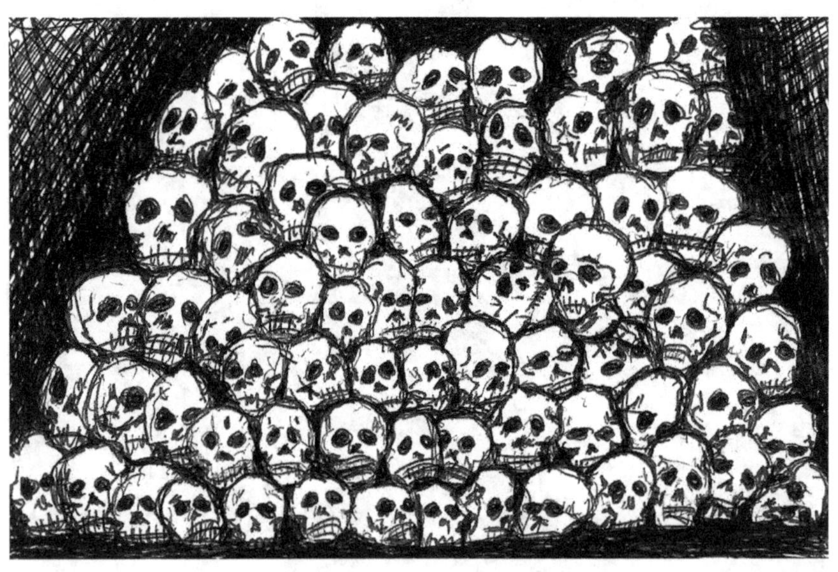

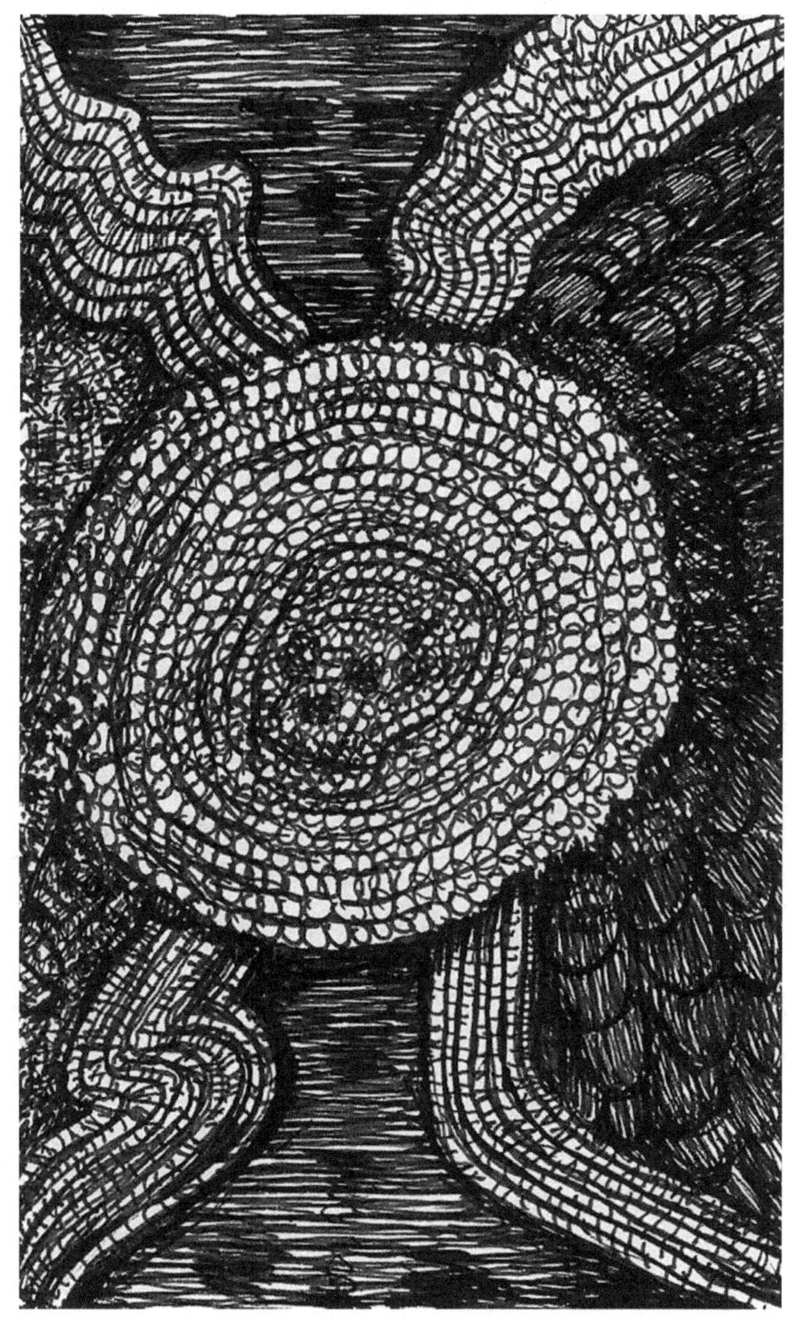

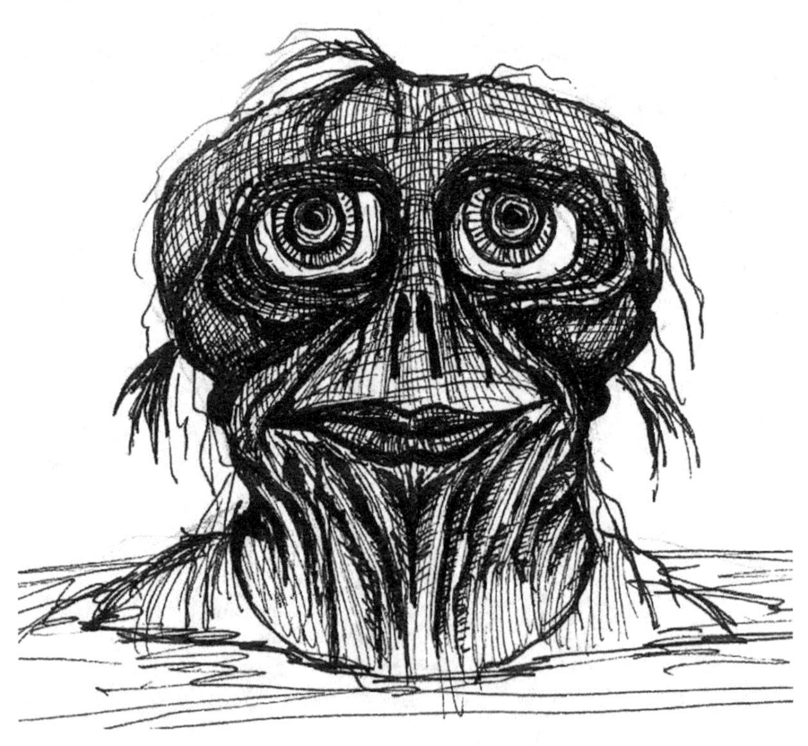

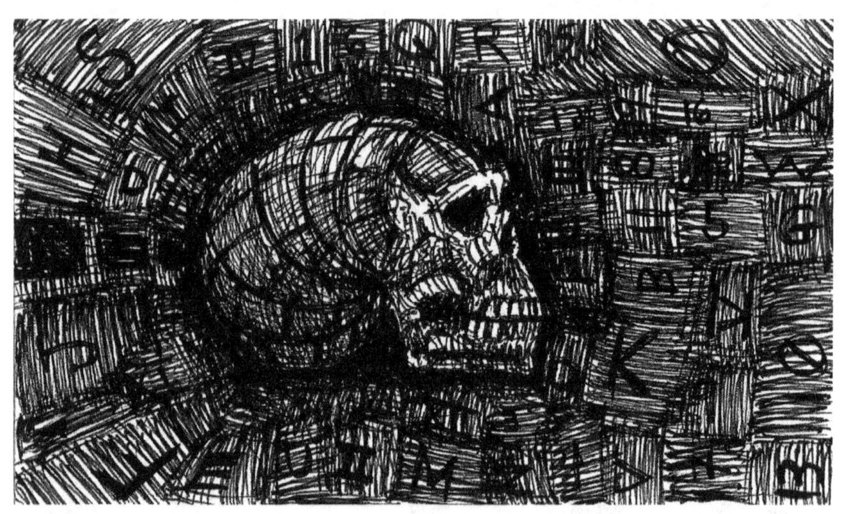

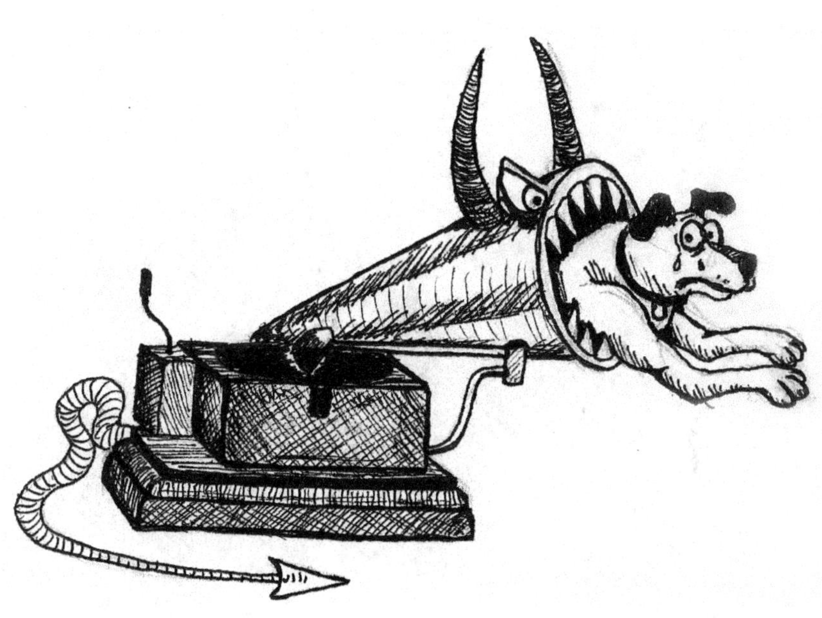

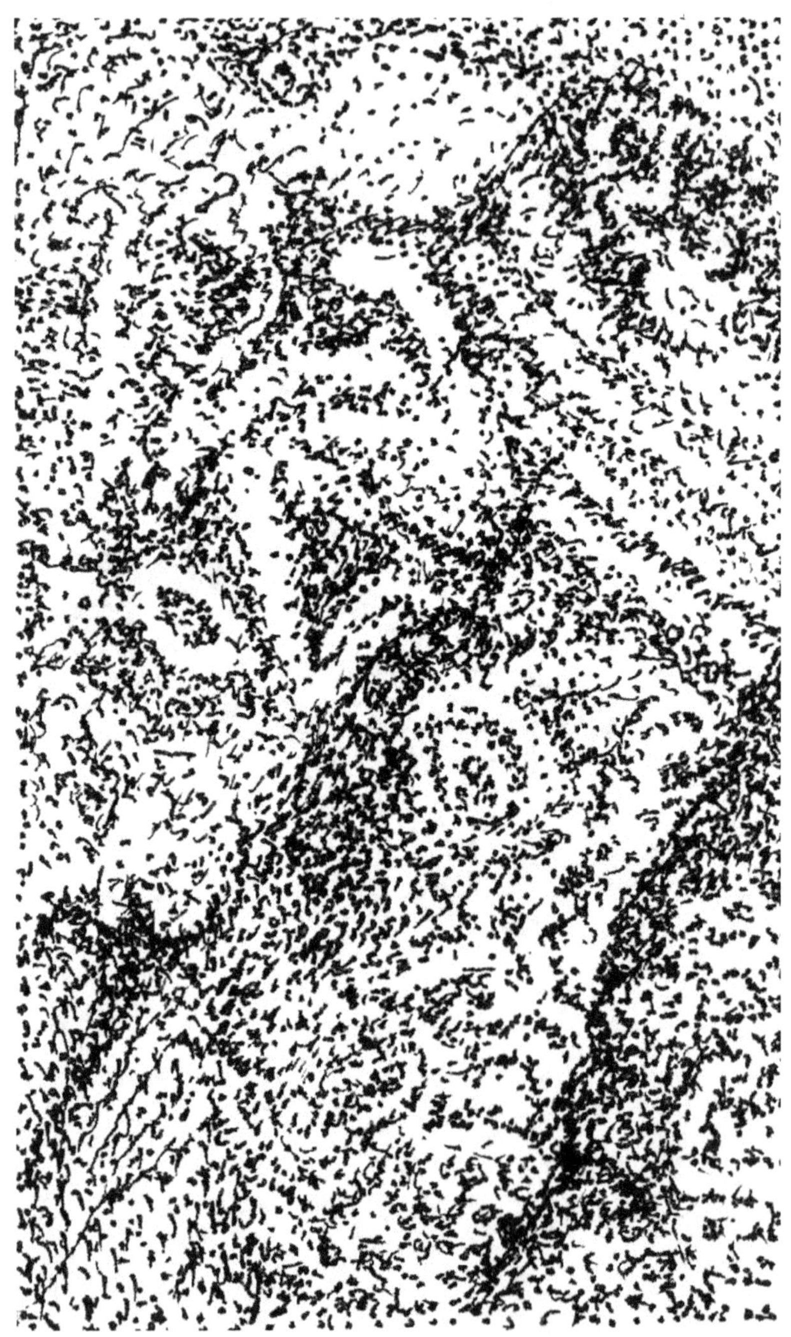

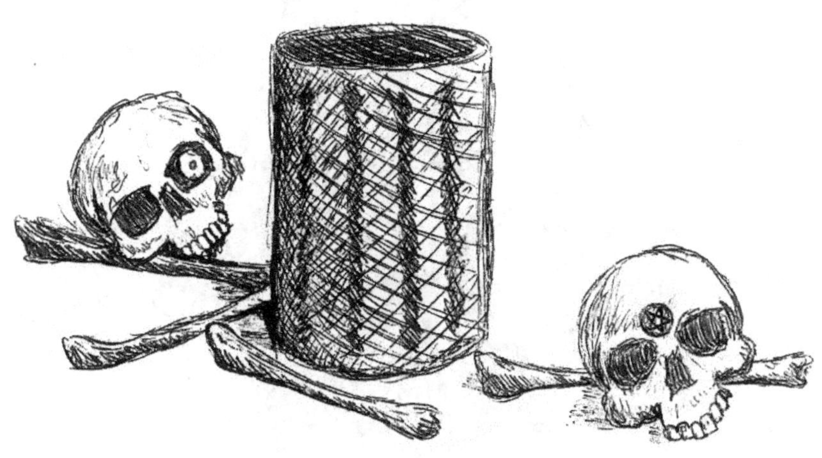

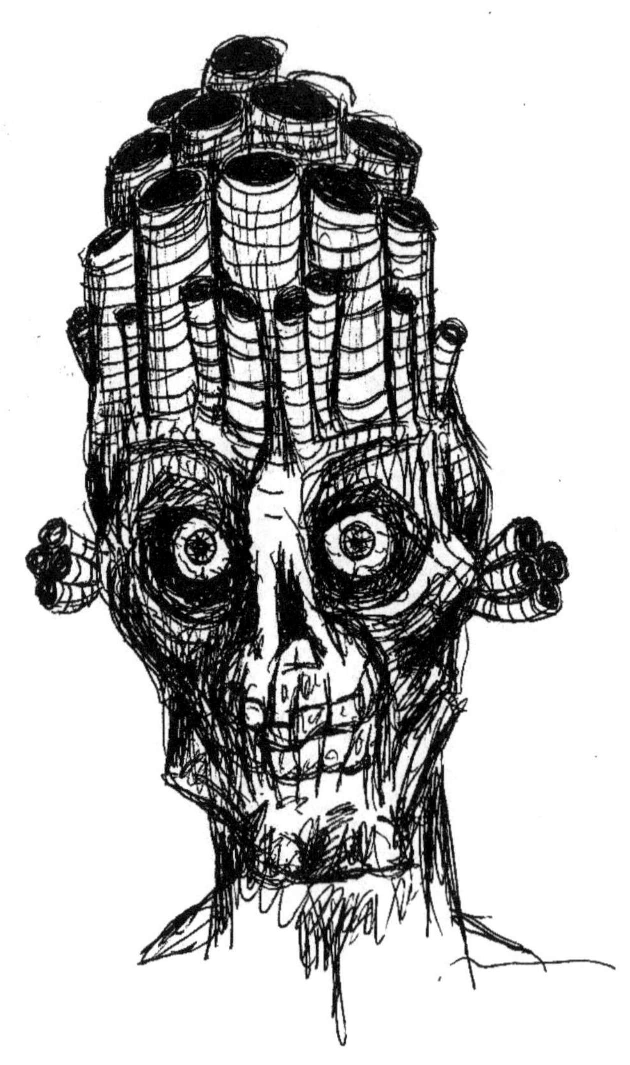

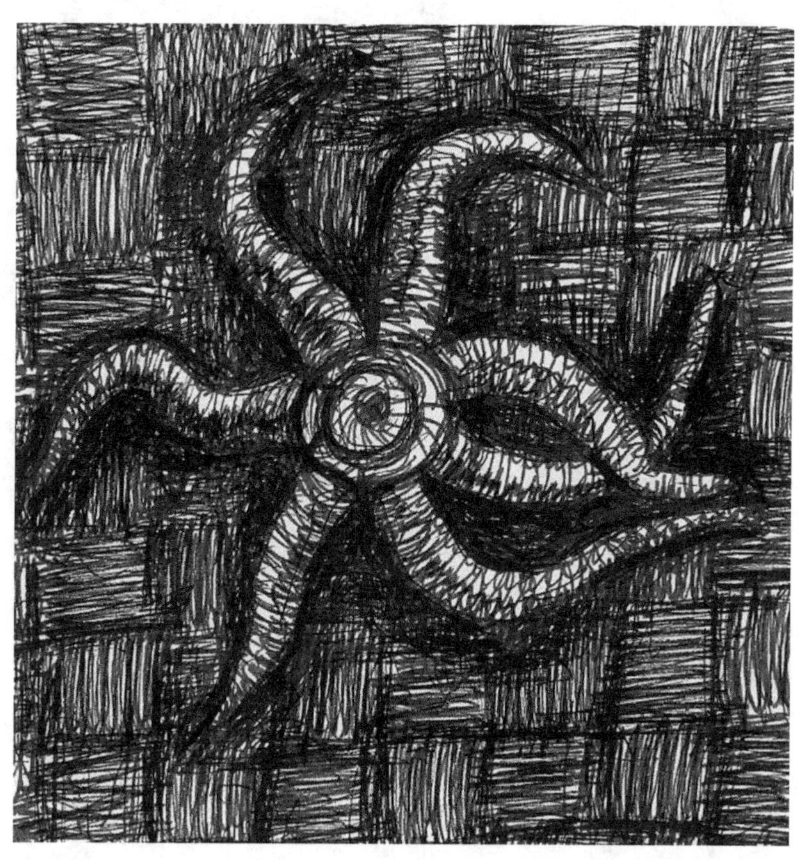

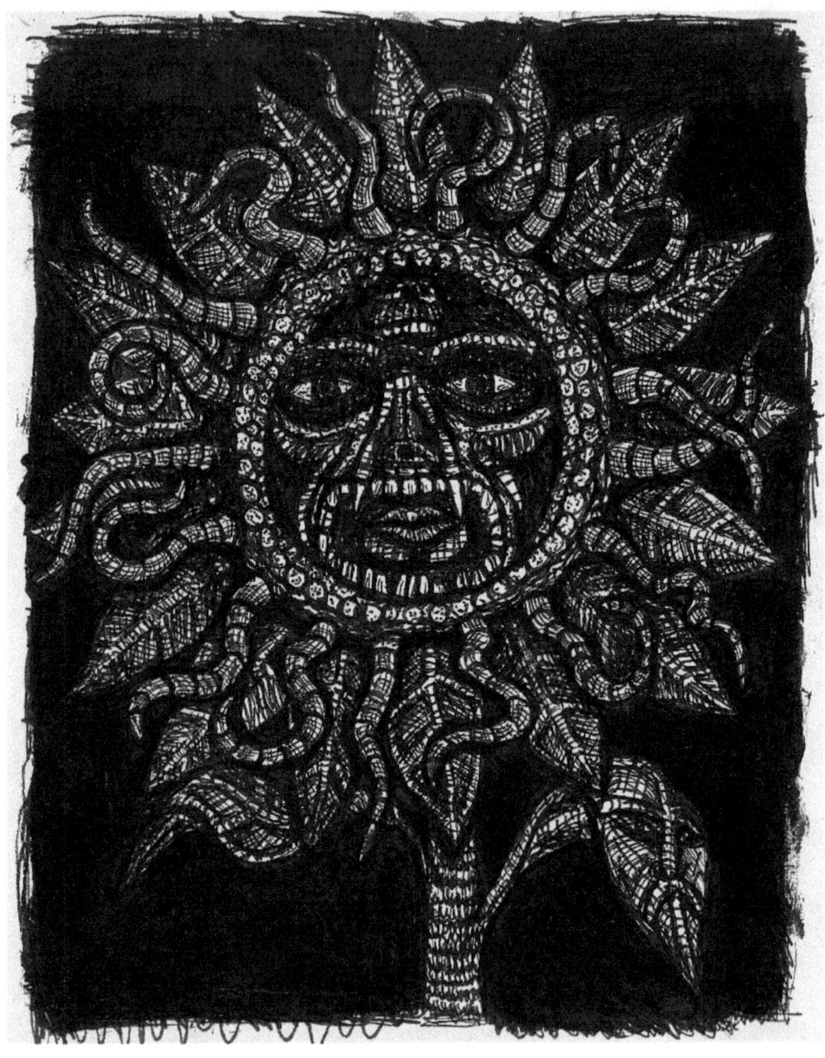

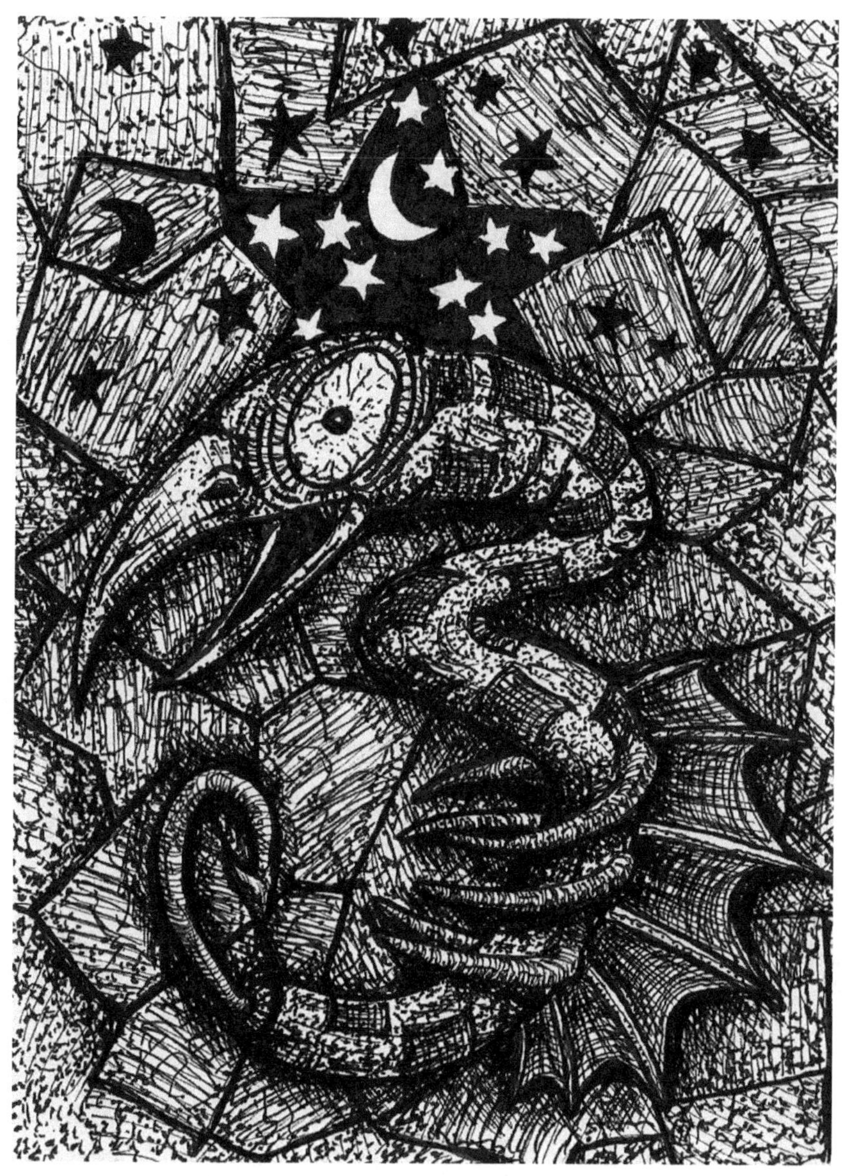

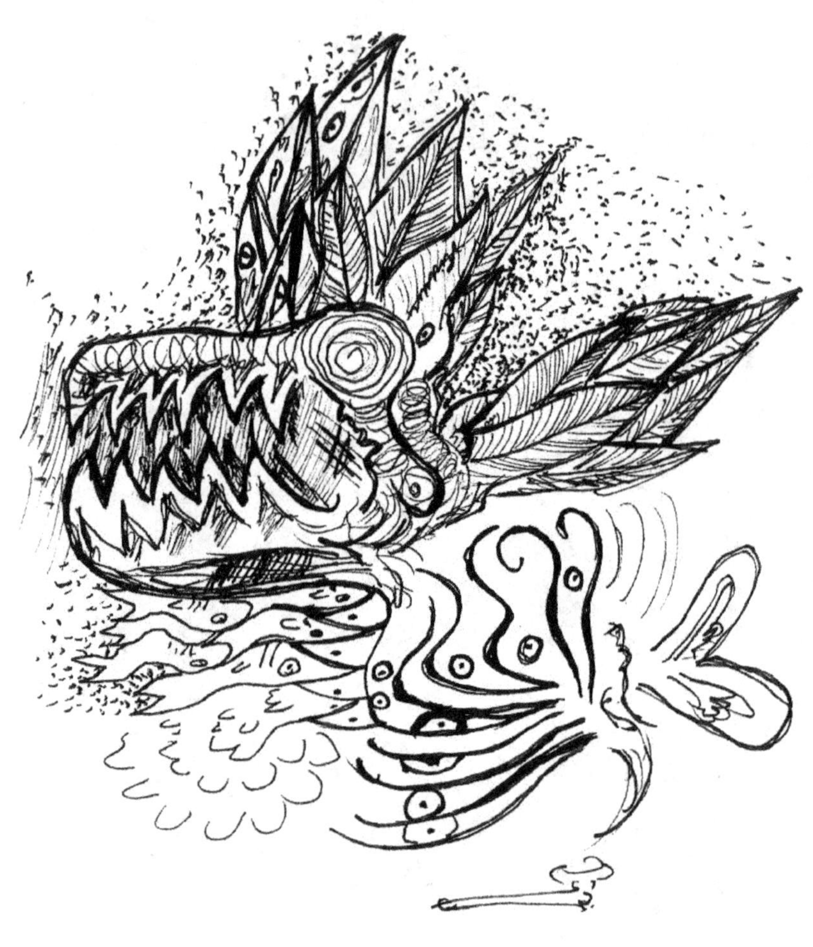

ELH

christiania
copenhagen Denmark

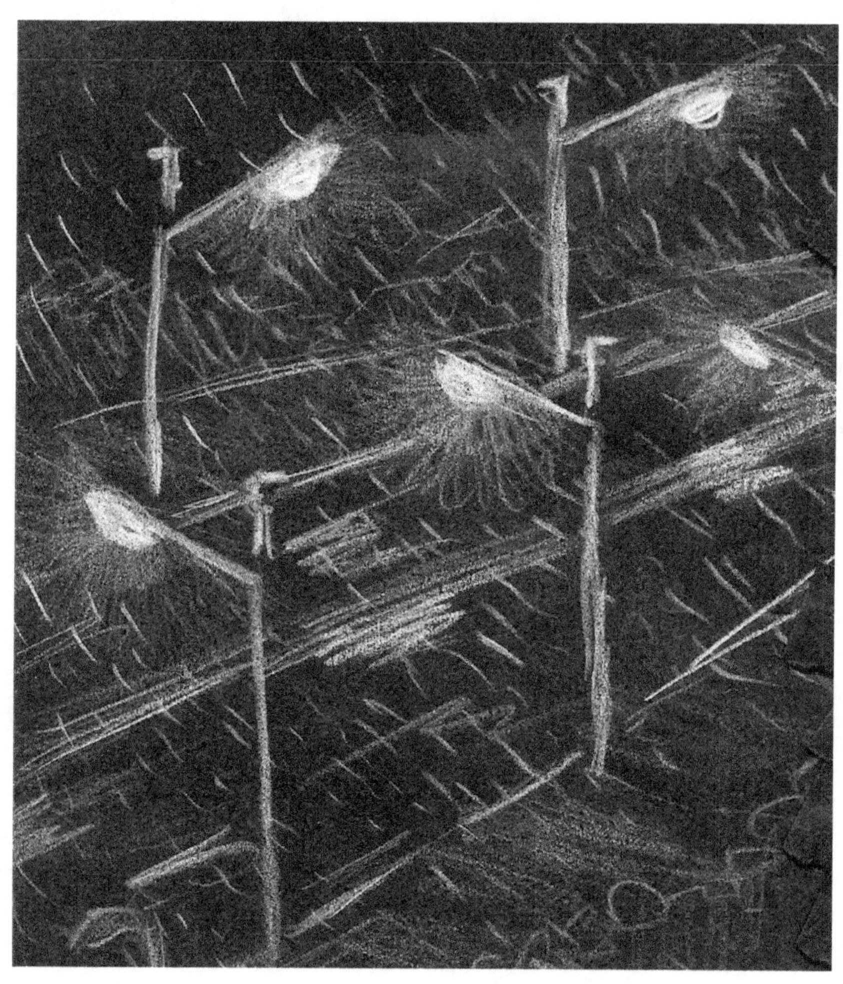

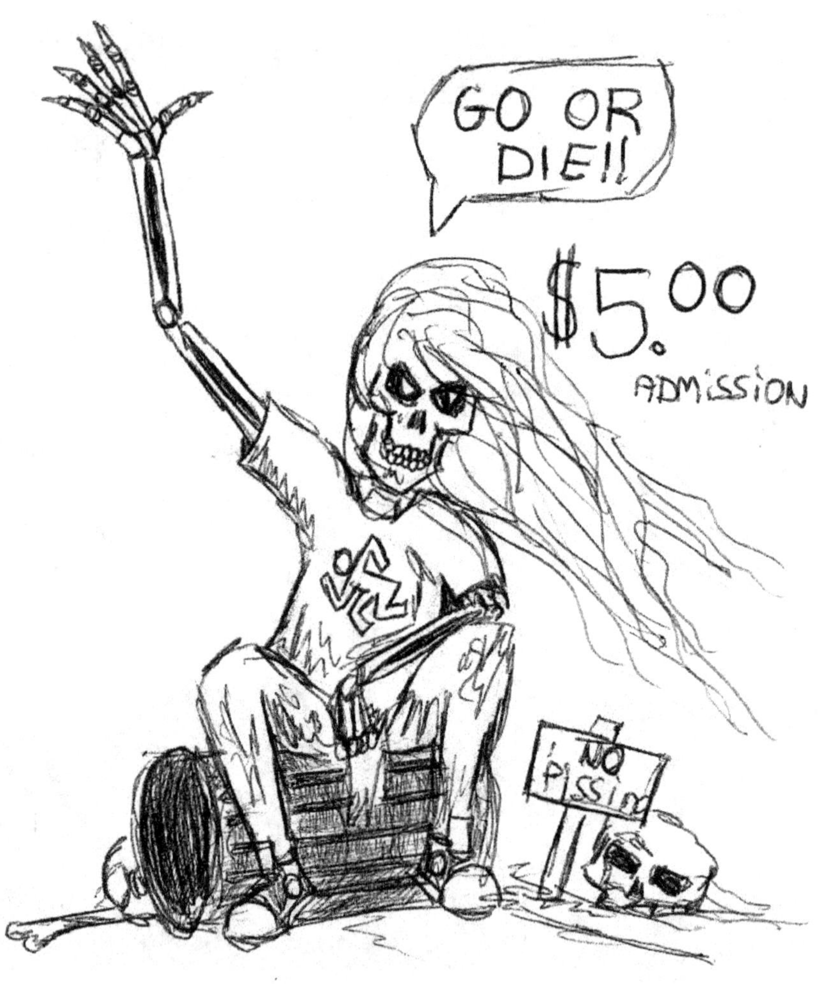
GO OR DIE!!
$5.00 ADMISSION
NO PISSIN

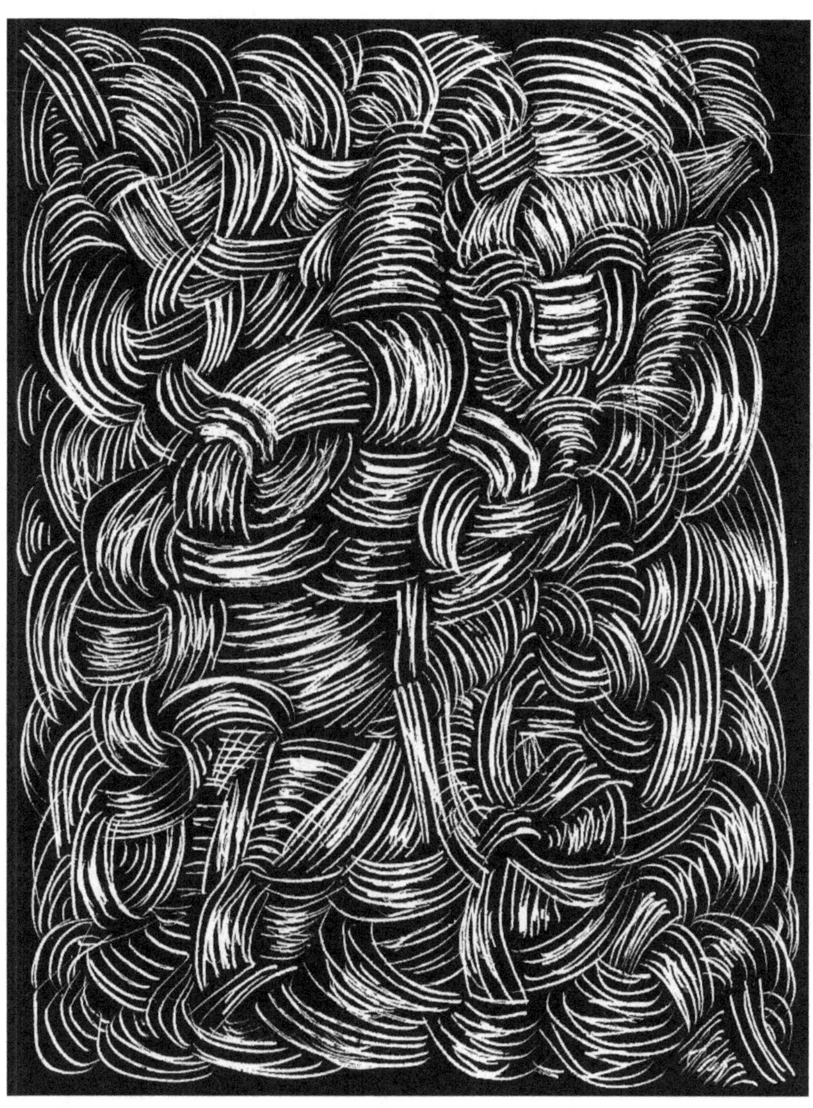

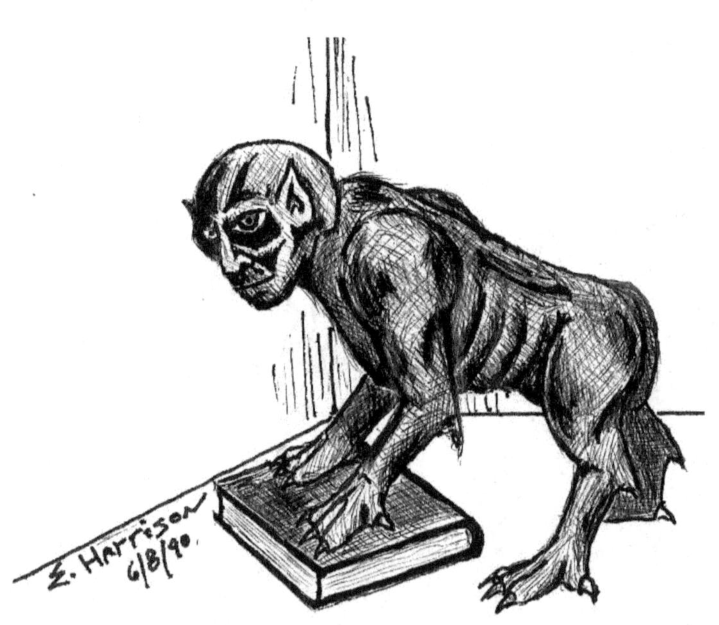
E. Harrison
6/8/90

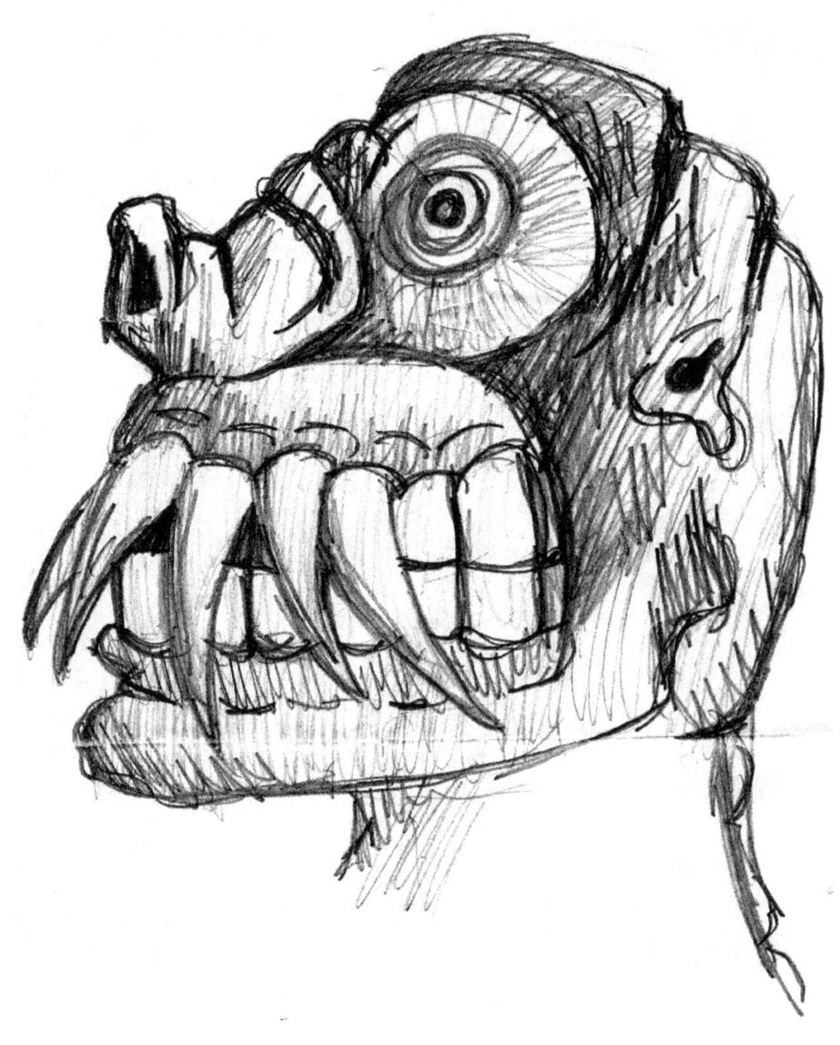

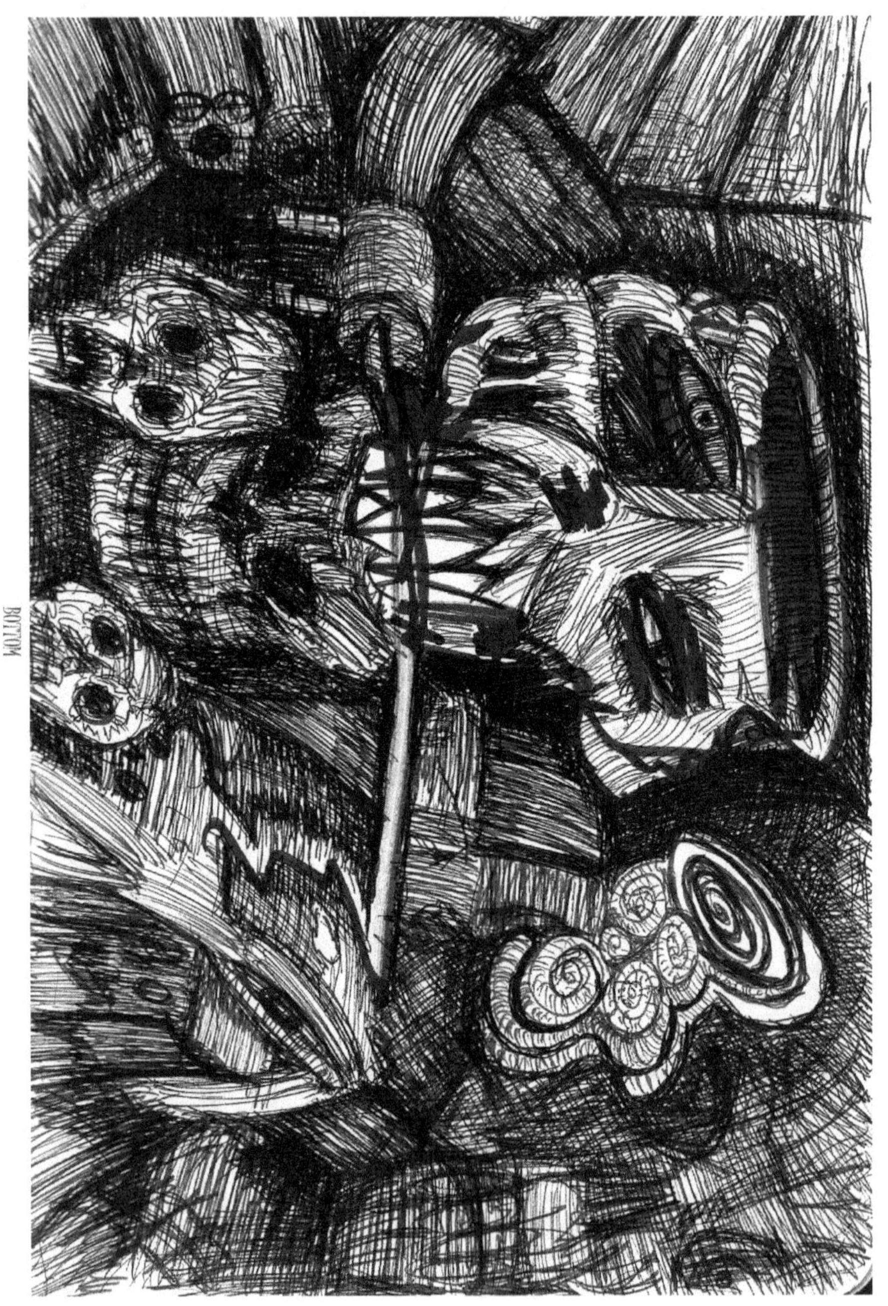

BOTTOM

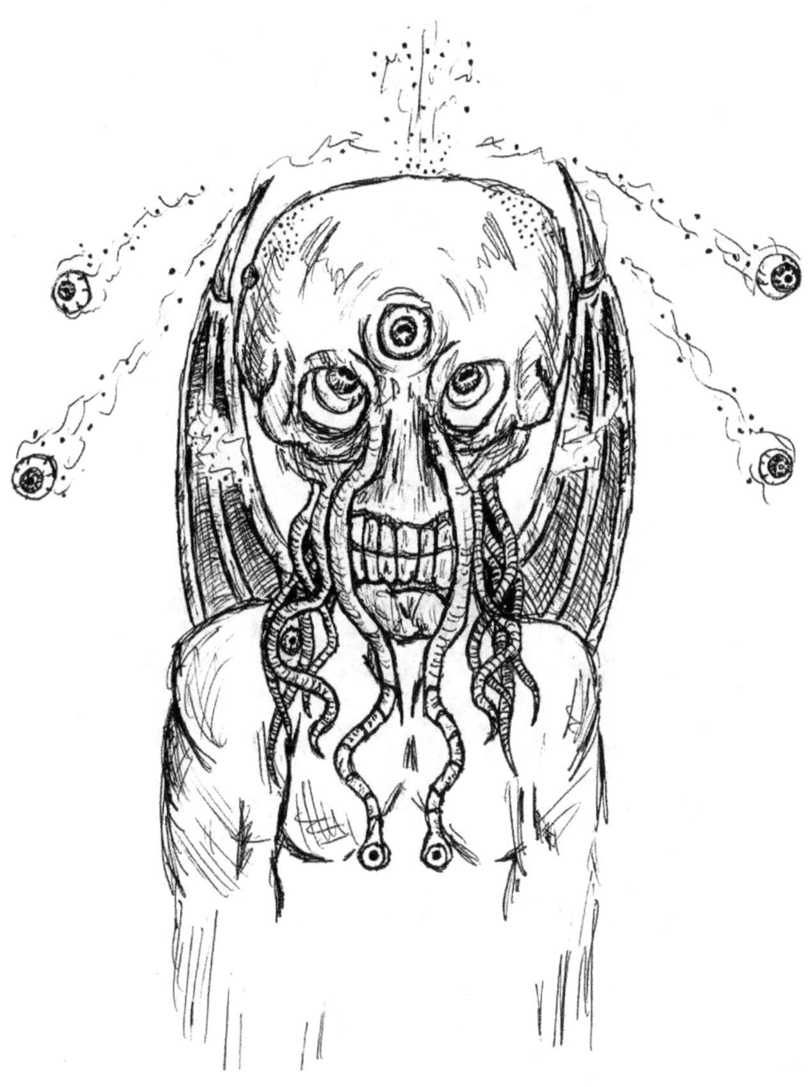

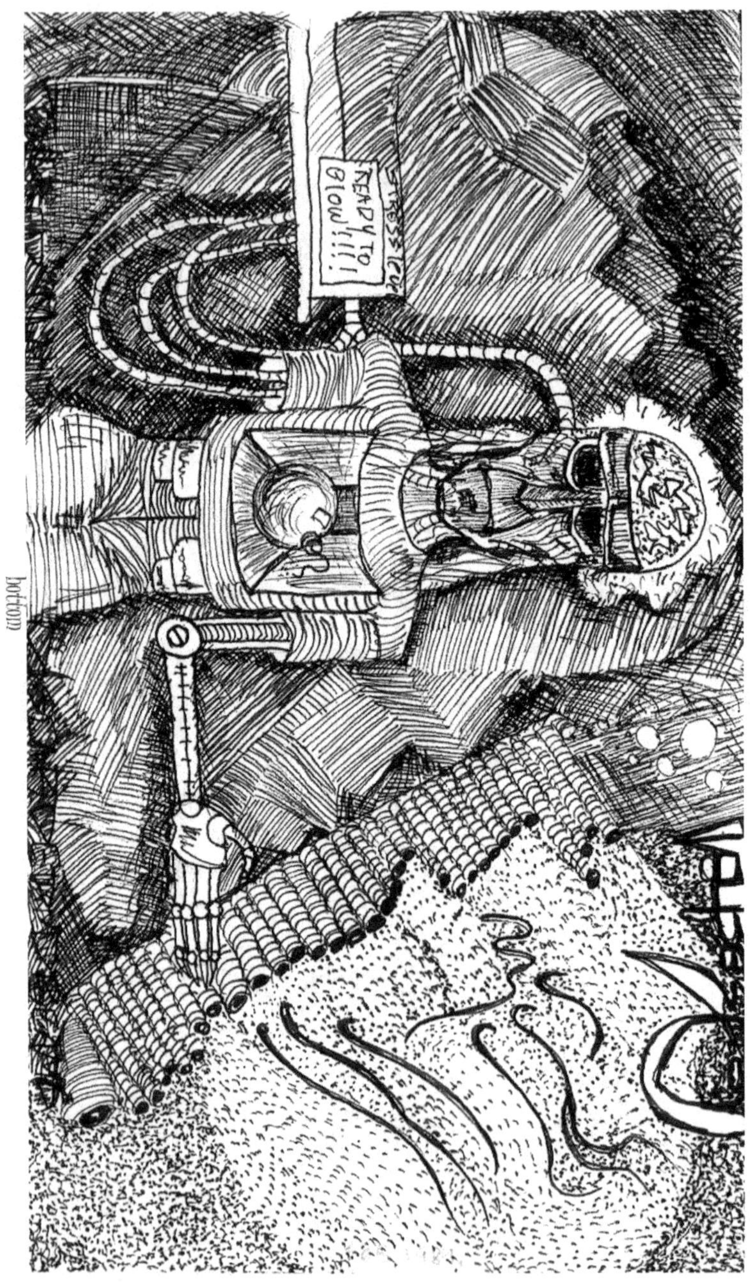

bottom

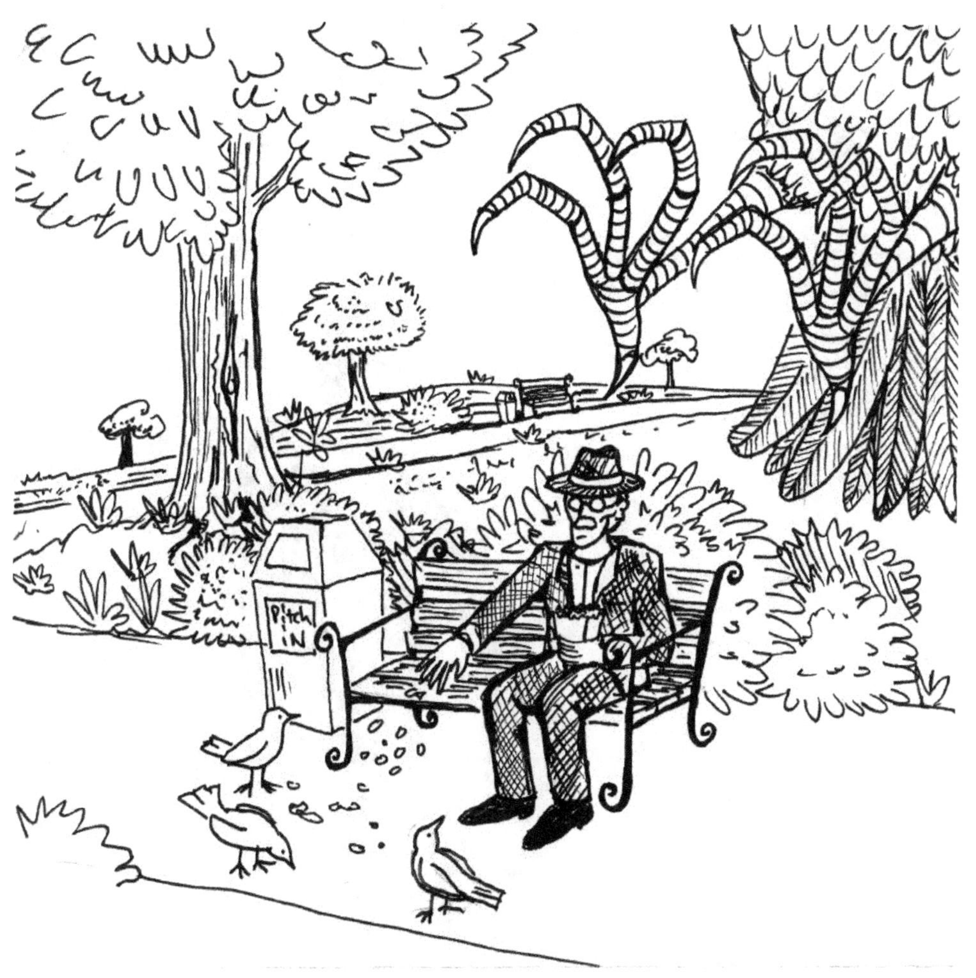
Pitch
IN

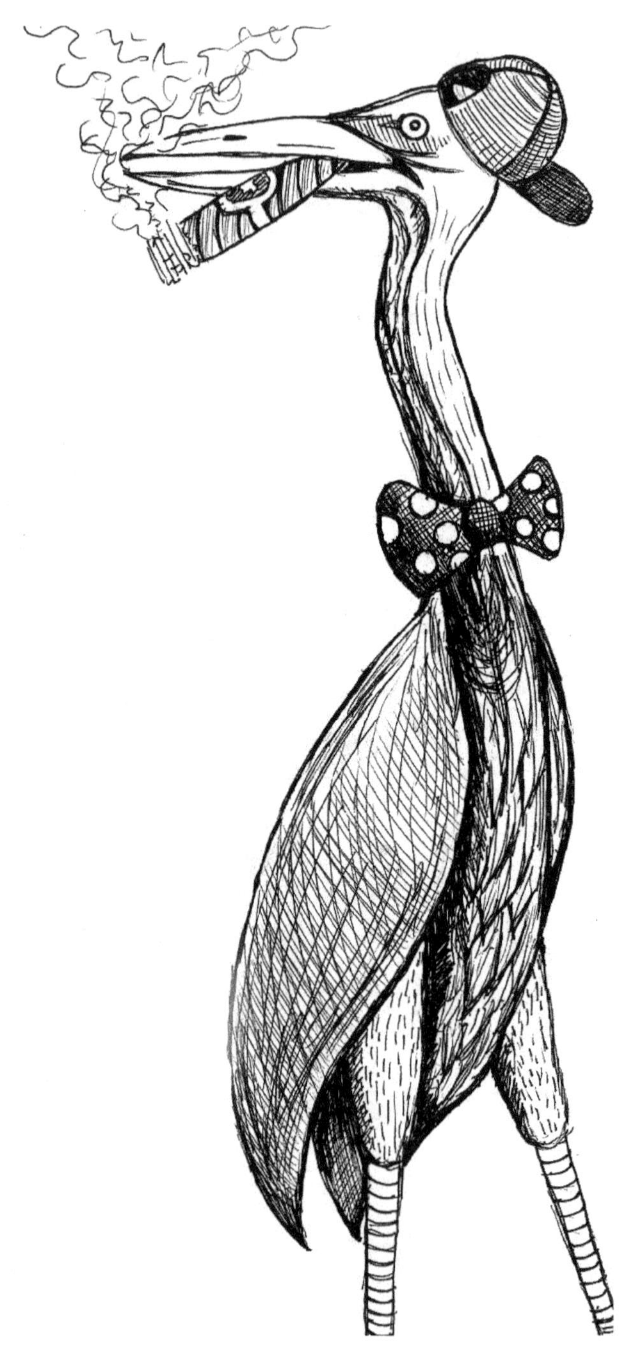

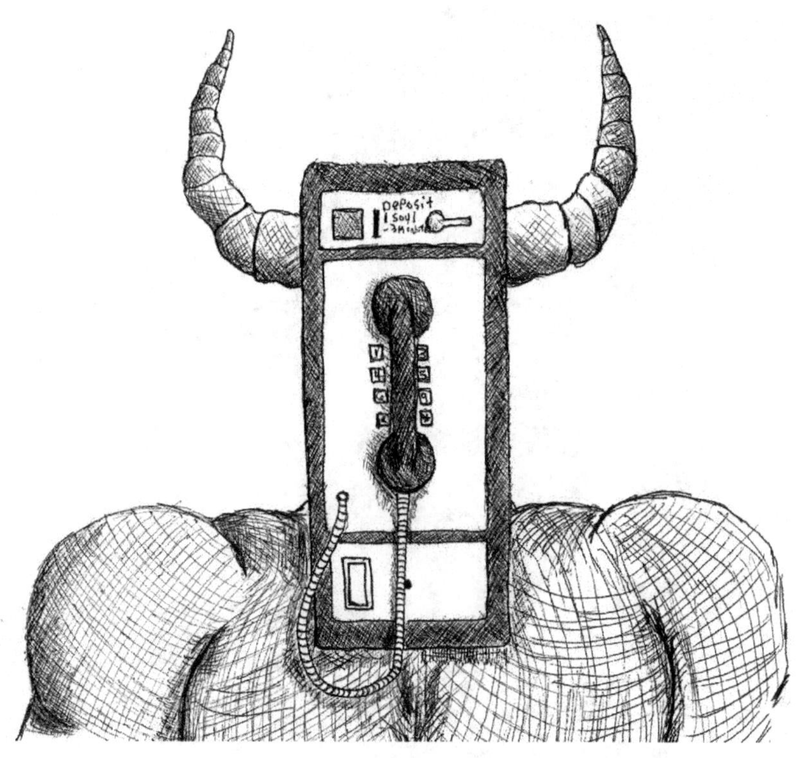
Deposit
1 soul

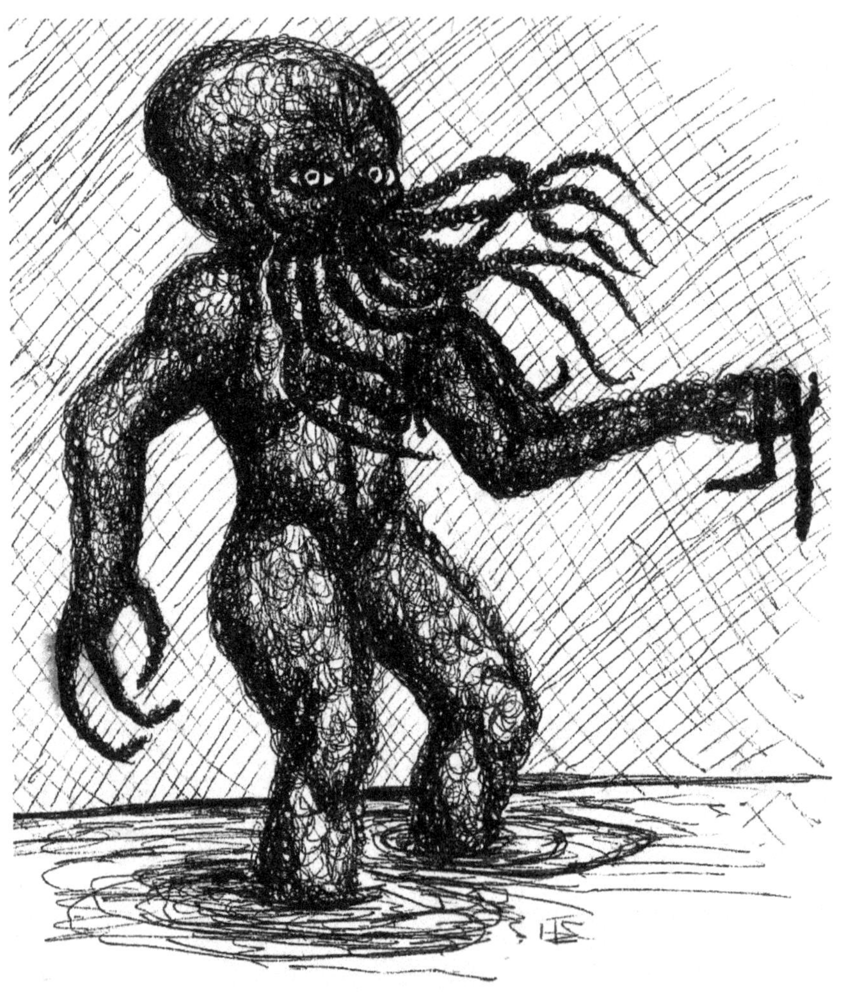

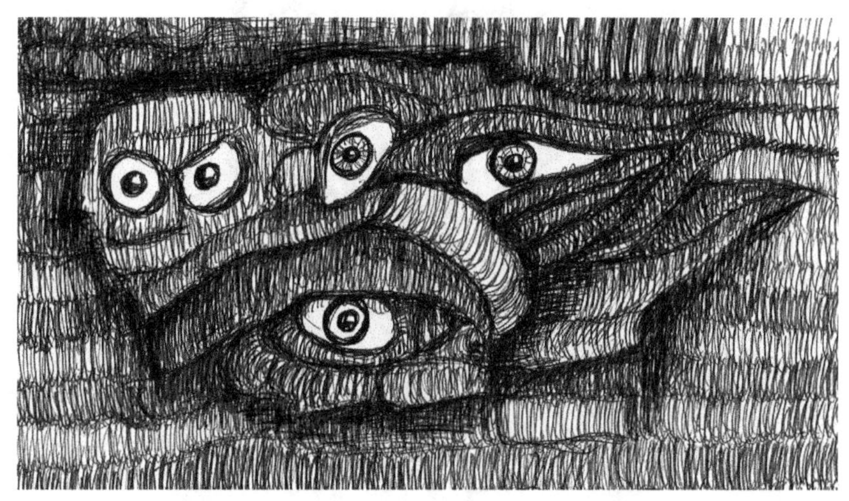

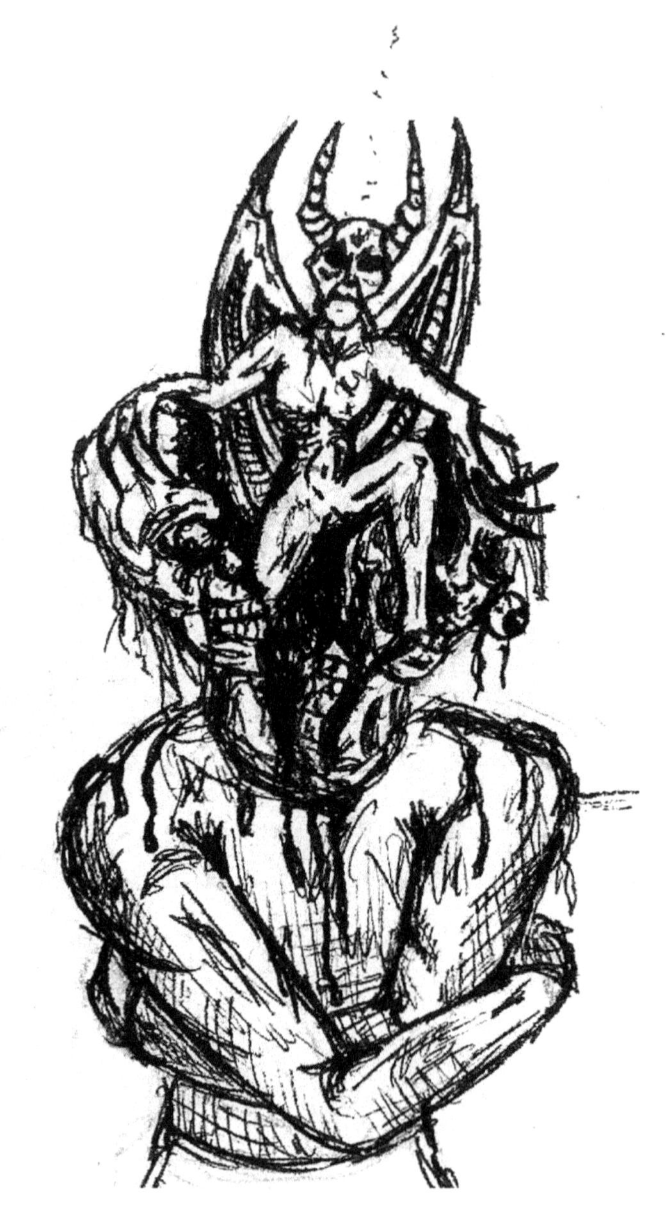

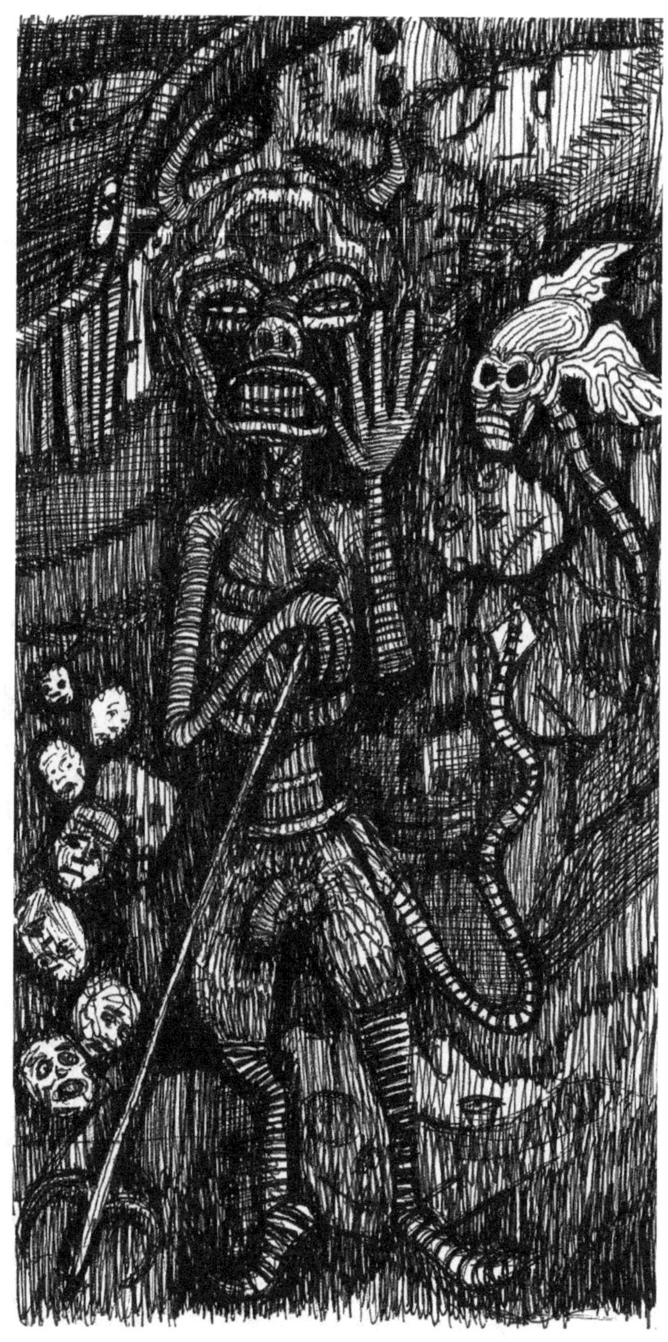

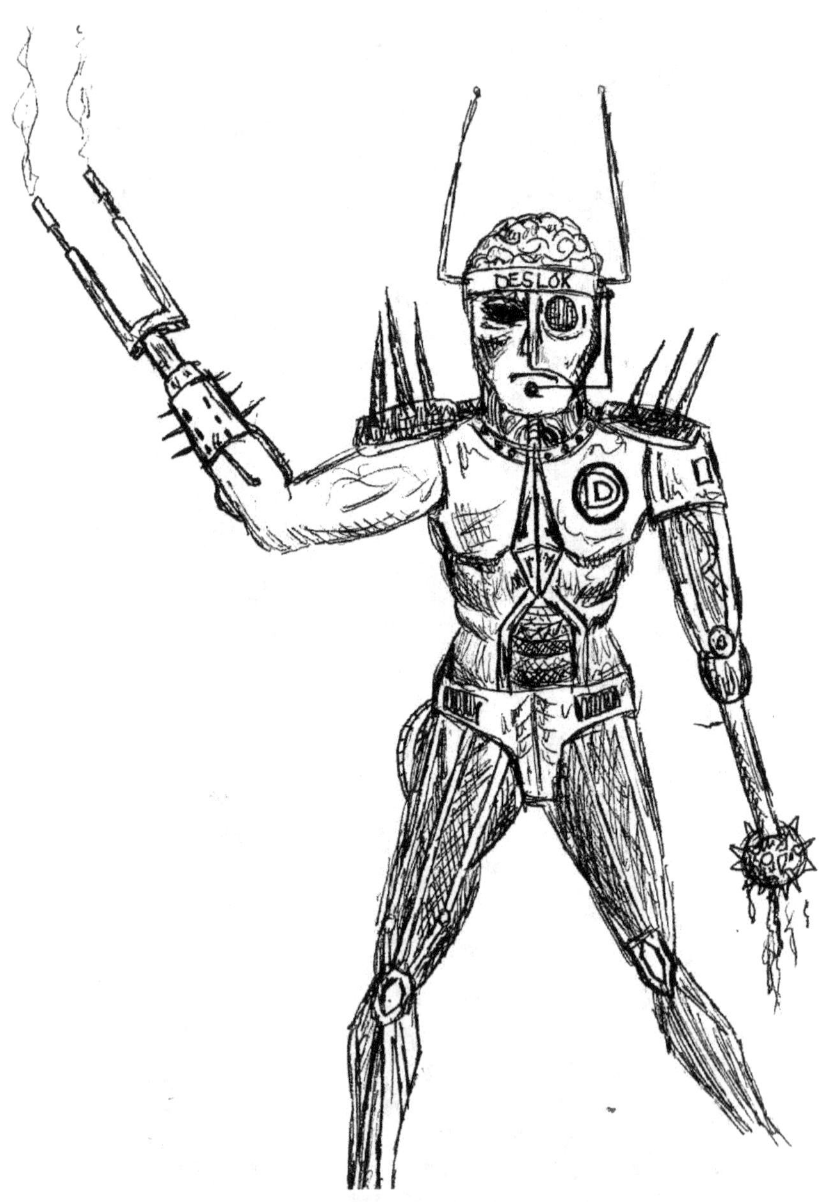
DESLOK

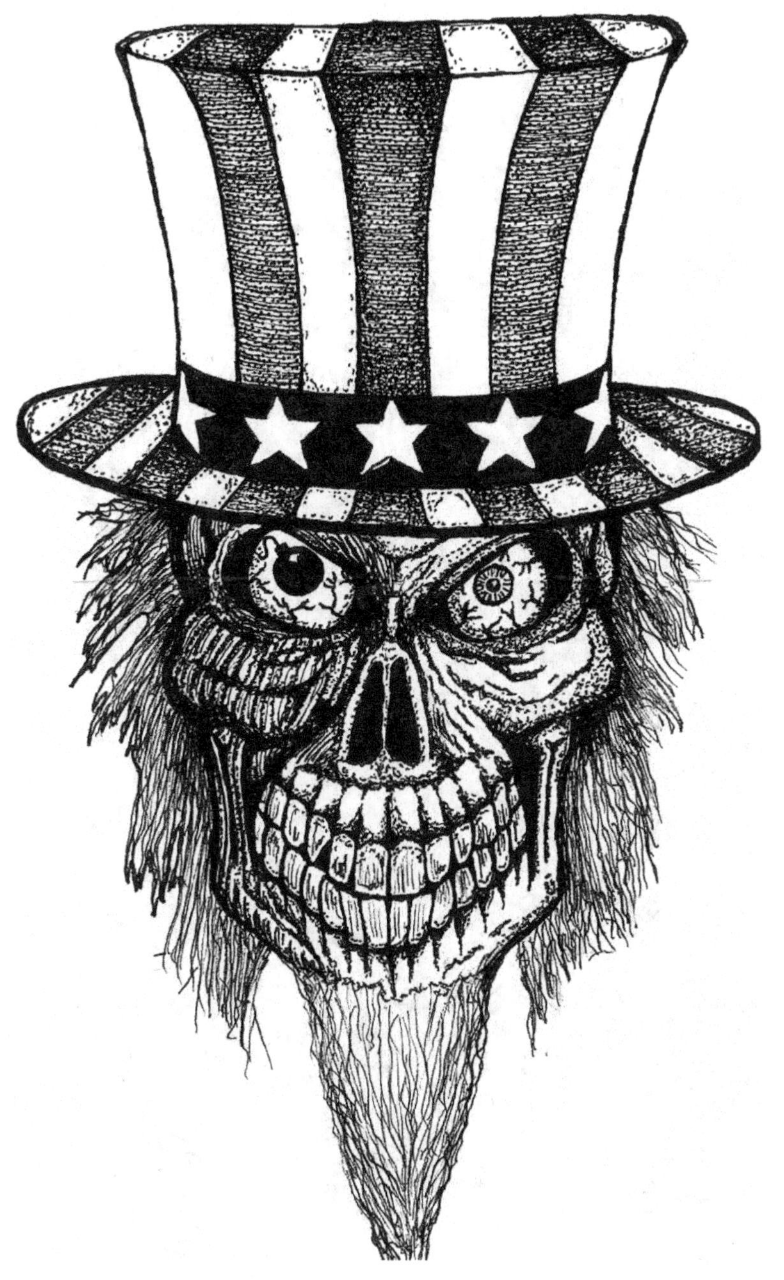

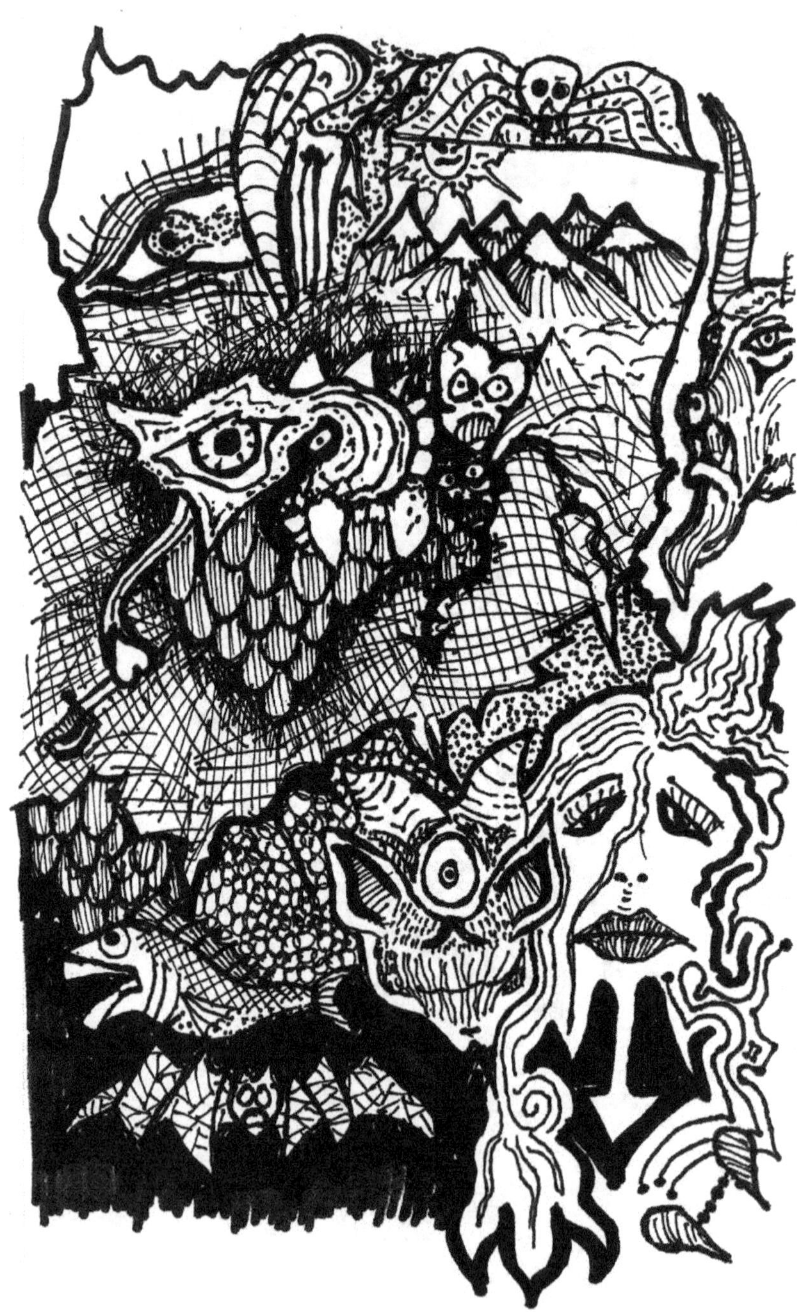

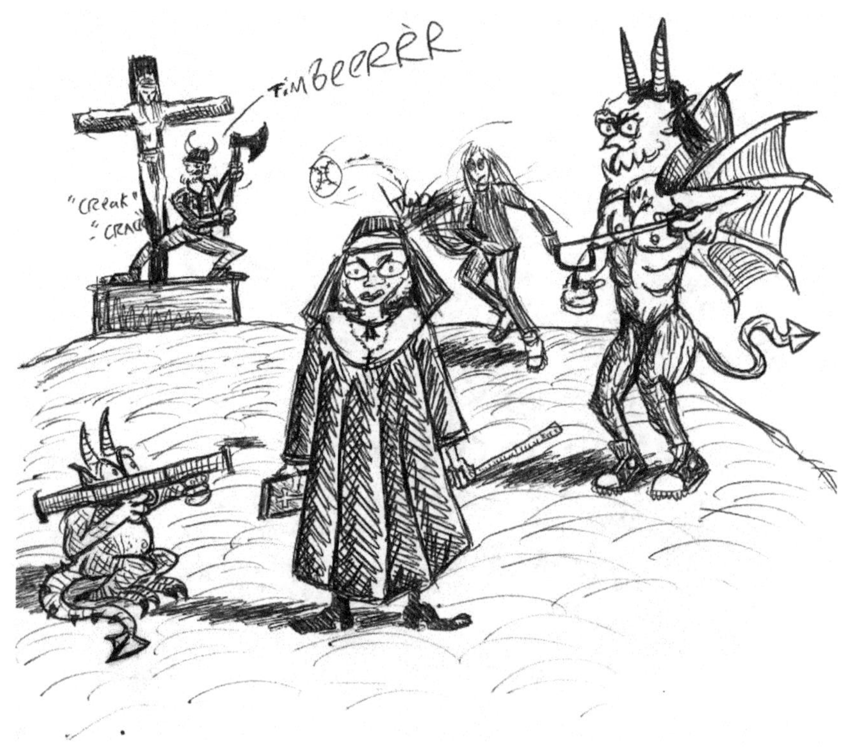
TIMBERRRR
"Creak"
"CRAC

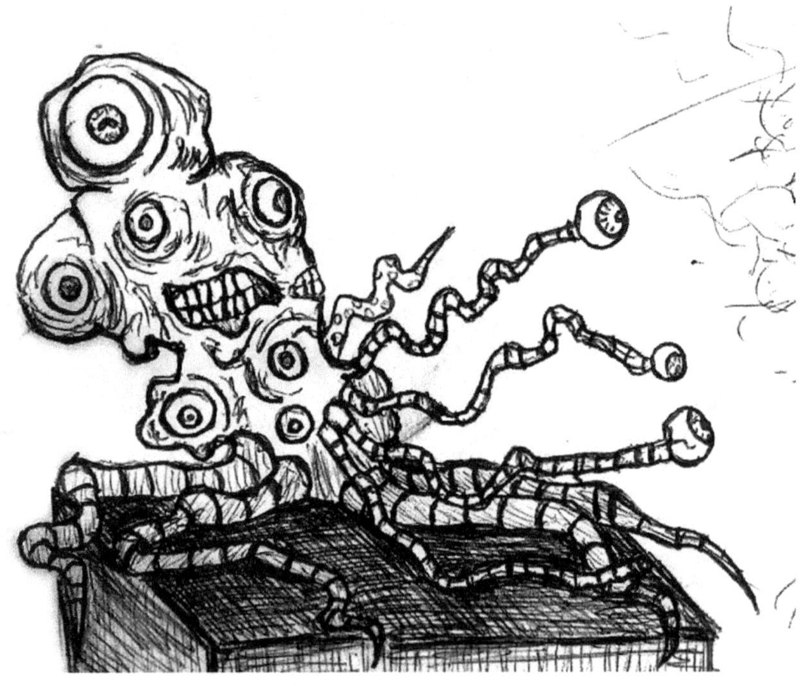

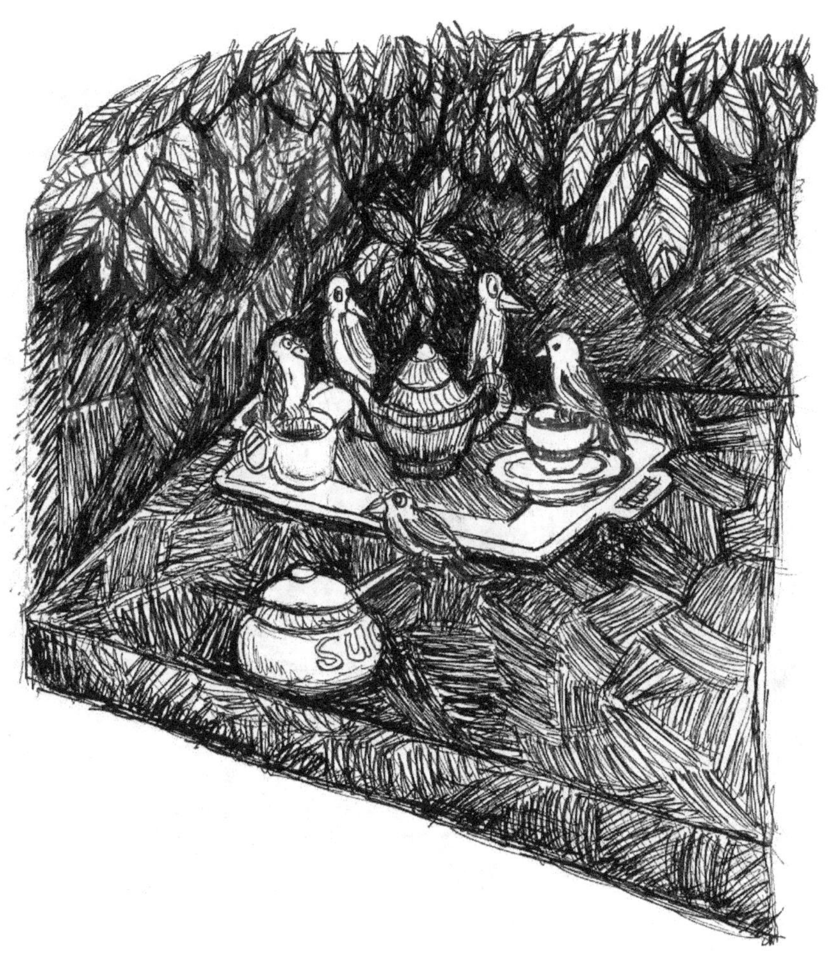
SU

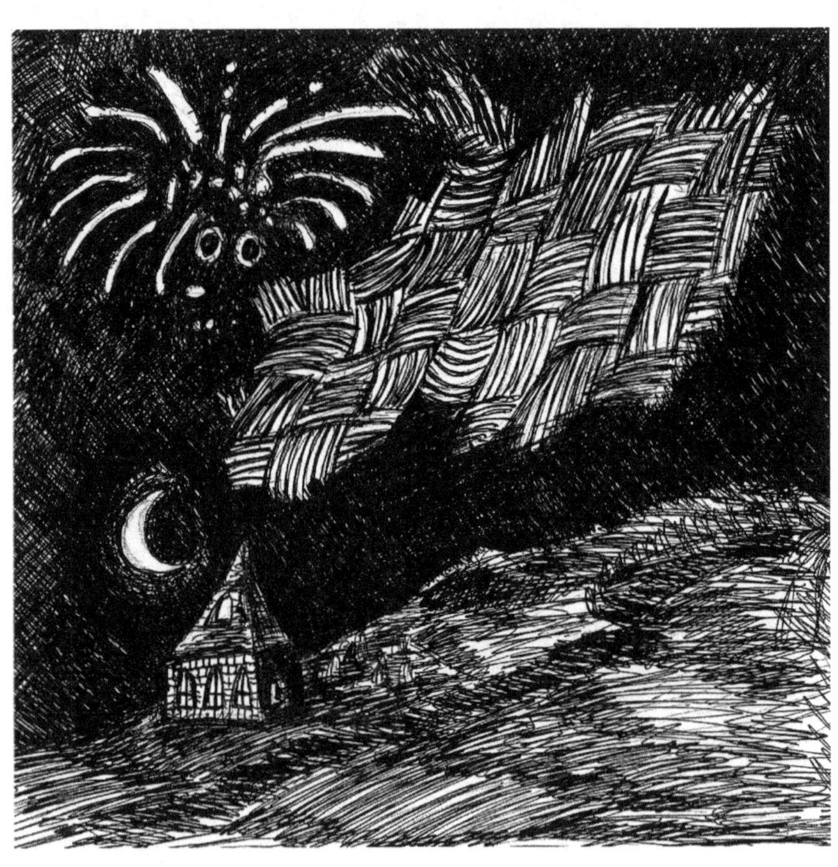

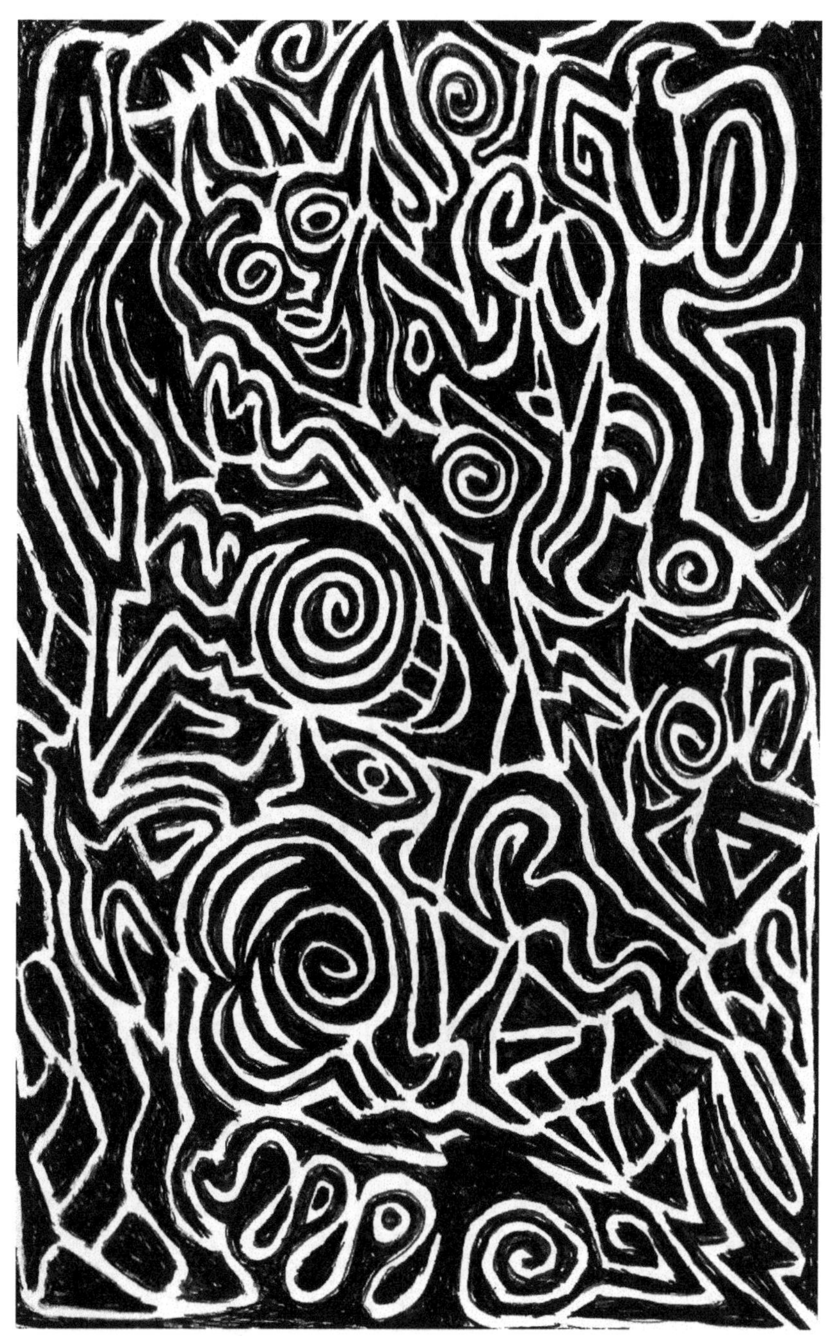

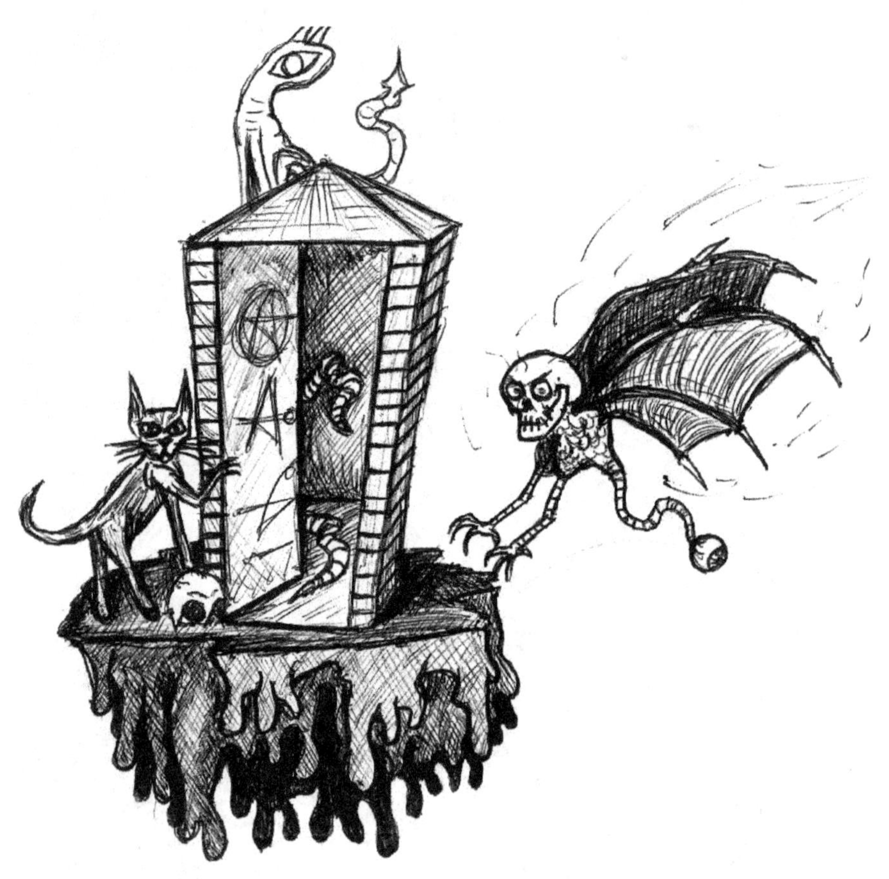

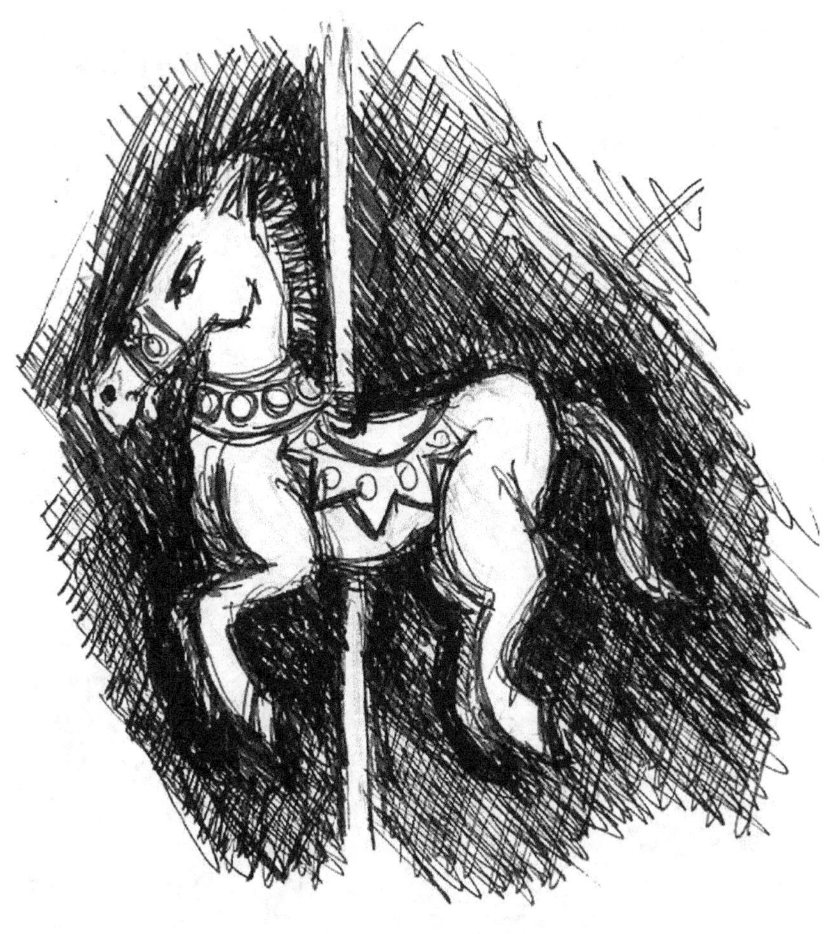

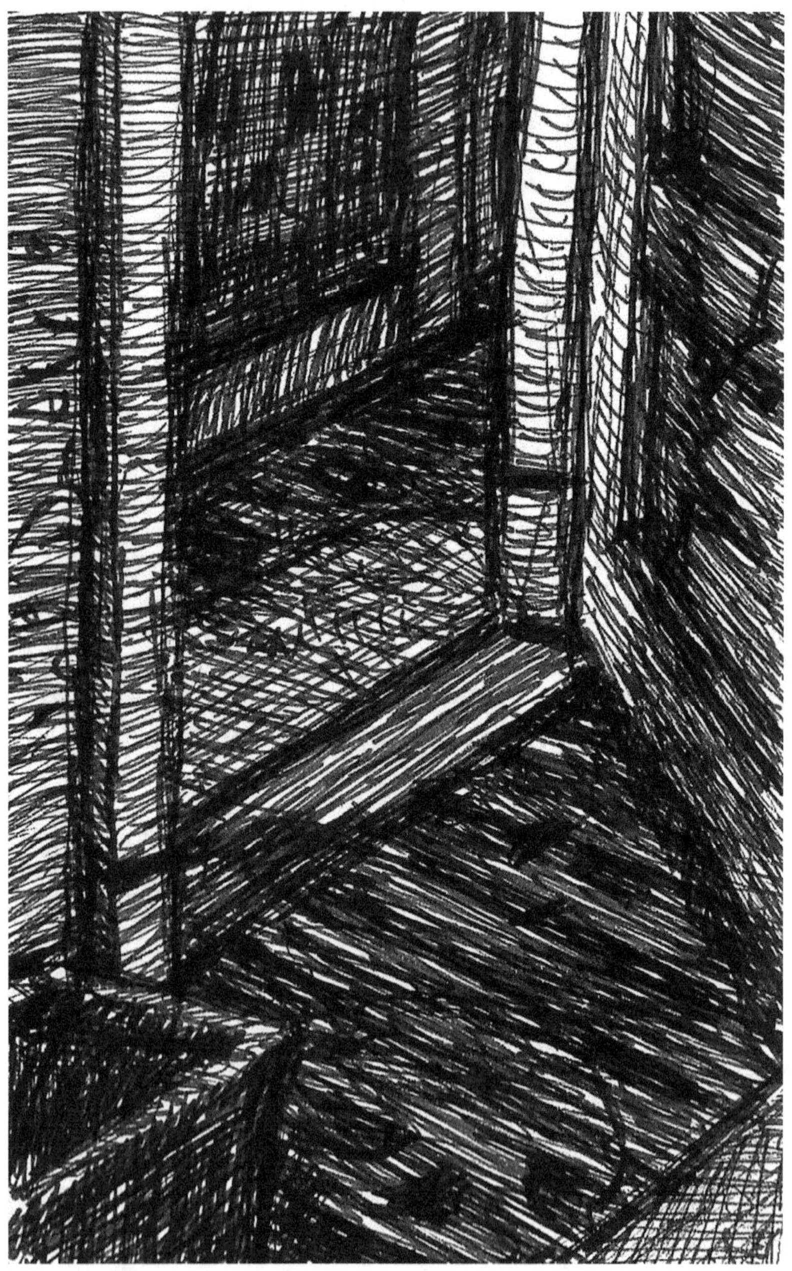

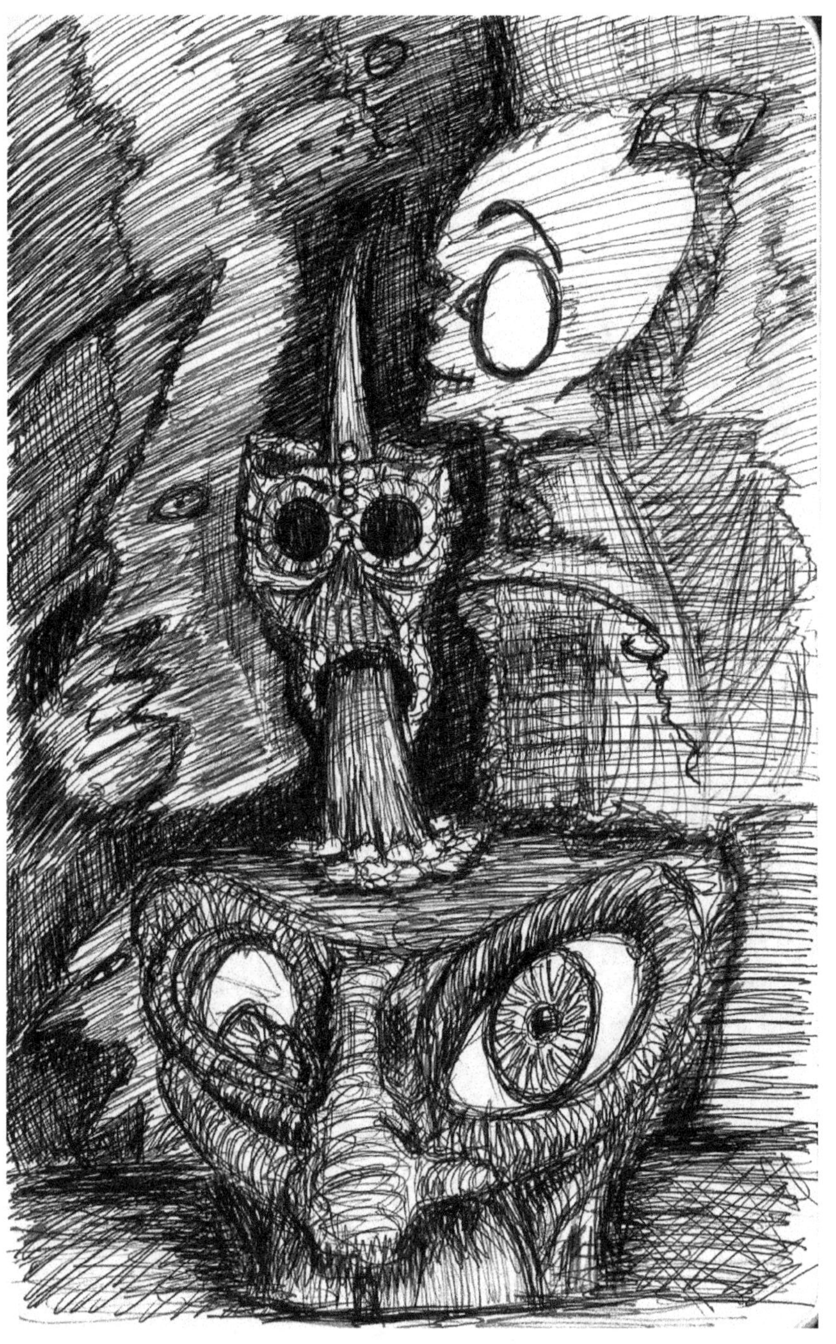

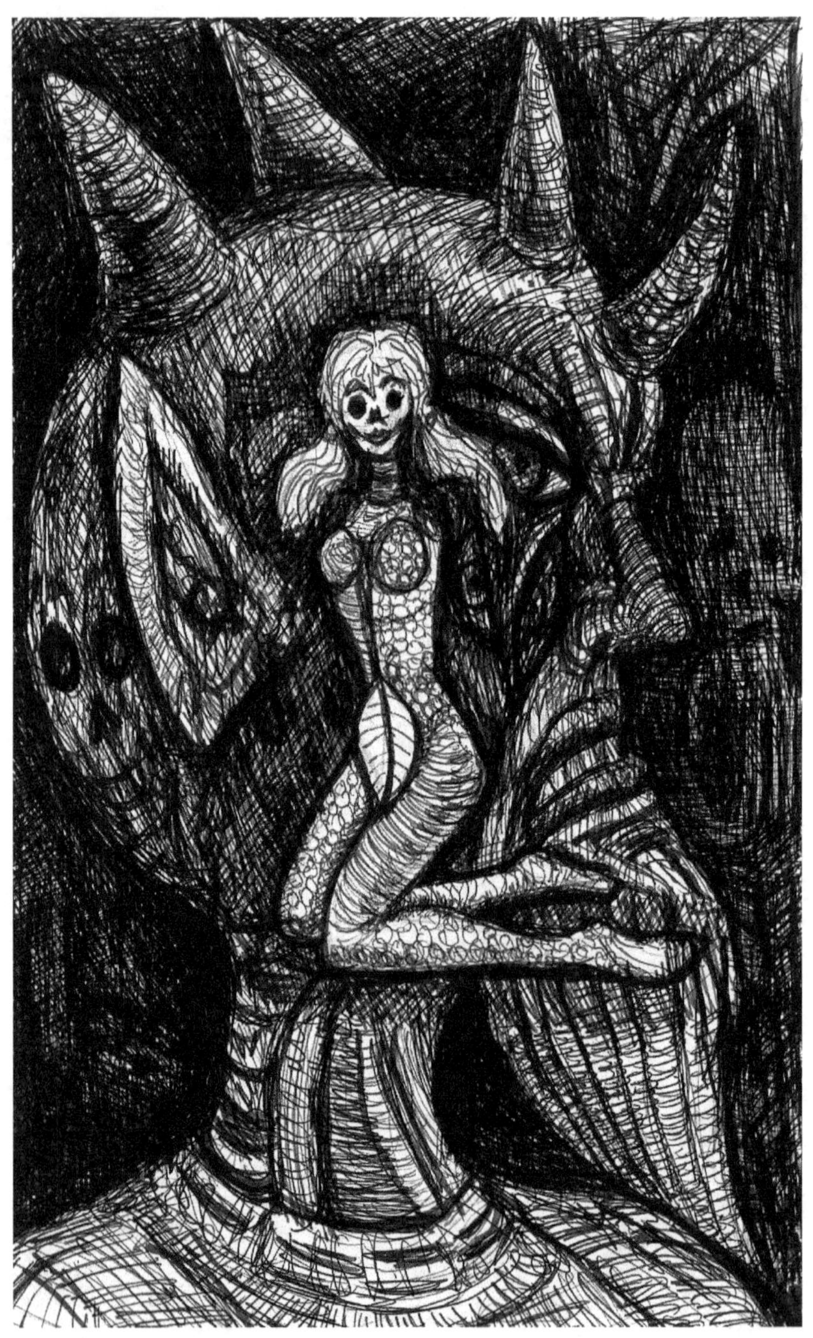

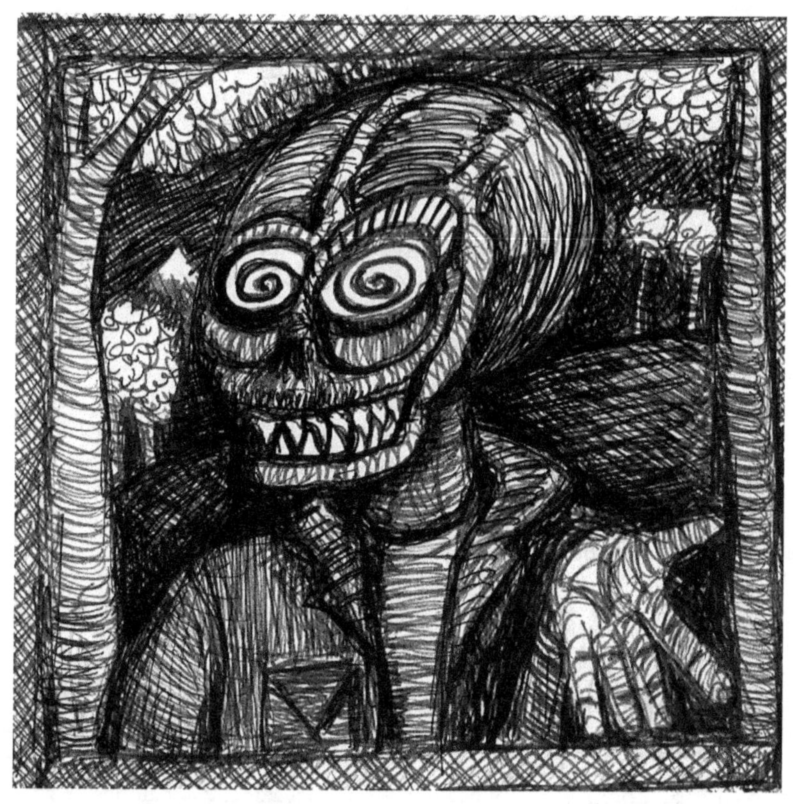

All of the pictures, cartoons, scribbles and doodles in this book were drawn by Eric C. Harrison, circa 1987-2012. A few have made prior appearances, which are listed on the next page.

Most of the drawings in this collection were done in black ink on index cards and small scraps of paper and have been stored in an old wooden treasure chest (guarded by giant, blood-thirsty shrews) for years.

A few of the images in this book were created on scratchboard. One of these scratchboard pieces was used as the cover for a book called Finding the Secret Sea by Eric C. Harrison & Mike Maguire, 2012.

"While I consider none of these pictures to be fantastic works of art, I do believe that they all have character." – Eric C. Harrison, 2012

Acknowledgments

pg 4 – "The Grundle" was used in various ways over the years, once appeared in Monkey Bite Magazine alongside a Grief interview.

Pg 15 - "bottle bat/addiction demon" – used by the band Fistula for t-shirts.

pg 12 – This was done in pipe-resin, paint and ink. Used as interior artwork for the CD "Burdened By Your Existence" by the band Fistula.

pg 16 - This sketch eventually became the painting used as interior art for the the album "Miserably Ever After" by Grief. The original is done in blue pen.

Pg 18, 19, 20 - These drawings appeared in the book "Parallel Enigmas" poems by Carter Monroe & Eric C. Harrison, Third Lung Press.

Pg 21 – A page from "Finding The Secret Sea" drawn while on the Newburyport/Rockport train, to curb paranoia.

pg 22 -"She Comes for Tea and Voodoo" This drawing is owned by the musician, Tori Amos.

pg 25 - Psychopomp # 2 - this was used by the band, Grief for t-shirts in 2008 for the Godless Yankee Invasion of Europe Tour.

pg 26 - Psychopomp # 3 - appeared in Boue Magazine, 2009 alongside a Grief interview done in Poitiers, France while on tour. Boue Magazine is published and circulated in France.

pg 35 – This is the raw cover art for "Finding The Secret Sea." done on scratch-board in 2012.

pg 52 - art for some flyer, circa 1990.

pg 59 - Demo tape cover for Chicken Chest & The Bird Boys, circa 1990

pg 60 - flyer art for the band, Radio Frequency Lesion, circa early 90's

pg 66 – unused sketch for a band I was in called, Deslok, circa late 80's

pg 67 - unused drawing for the band Democracide, circa 1990

pg 68 - done in a van while on tour with Grief, circa 1998

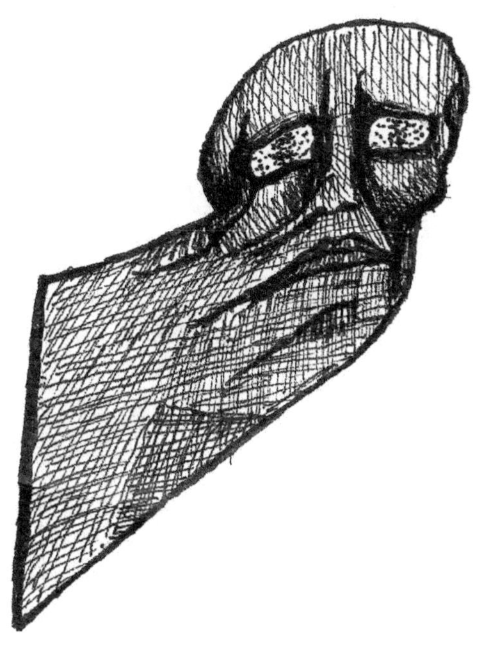

For information
Contact Eric C. Harrison

at

stilldiseased@aol.com

visit

www.marshpawpress.com

check out marsh-paw press on facebook

www.facebook.com/marshpawpress

www.ingramcontent.com/pod-product-compliance
Lightning Source LLC
LaVergne TN
LVHW010941110826
845149LV00013B/2706
9780988804029